The Silent Song of
MARY ELEANOR

The Silent Song of
MARY ELEANOR

Marjorie Wilkins Campbell

Western Producer Prairie Books
Saskatoon, Saskatchewan

Cover design by John Luckhurst/GDL

Cover photograph by "Photographer to Their Royal Highnesses the Prince and Princess of Wales, Duke of Edinburgh and Duke of Cambridge"

Author photograph by Rene Schoepflin

Printed and bound in Canada by Modern Press ⋯1
Saskatoon, Saskatchewan

The publisher acknowledges the support received for this publication from the Canada Council.

Western Producer Prairie Books publications are produced and manufactured in the middle of western Canada by a unique publishing venture owned by a group of prairie farmers who are members of Saskatchewan Wheat Pool. From the first book in 1954, a reprint of a serial originally carried in the weekly newspaper, *The Western Producer*, to the book before you now, the tradition of providing enjoyable and informative reading for all Canadians is continued.

Canadian Cataloguing in Publication Data

Campbell, Marjorie Wilkins, 1902–
     The silent song of Mary Eleanor

ISBN 0-88833-113-4

1. Wilkins, Mary Eleanor, 1873-1915.
2. Pioneers — Saskatchewan — Biography.
I. Title.
FC3522.1.W54C3 1983   971.24′02′0924
F1072.W54C3 1983   C83-091371-8

Contents

Foreword

The hardships of prairie settlement on remote homesteading quarter sections are a familiar strand in Canadian literature. In *The Silent Song of Mary Eleanor,* by the skillful use of a found diary, family letters, her father's recollections, and her own childhood recall, Marjorie Wilkins Campbell bears witness to what seven years of adventure in the Qu'Appelle area of Saskatchewan did to the Wilkins family.

This book is a biography in the shape of a novel. It might as easily have been presented as fiction. But that would have detracted from the veracity essential to the deep sympathy the reader comes to feel for the slender English girl, caught up in her husband's dream of owning his own land. If the harshness is here, from the sod-roofed house buckling under its weight of snow, the fearful isolation, the repeated pregnancies, the assaults of winter storms and late summer prairie fires which could destroy a year's labor, so are the moments of beauty: fields of flax shining in the sun, the limitless prairie on a fine summer's day, the marvelous recapture of longed-for music on an early gramophone, which plays a symbolic part in the last scene of the story.

That period of our history now seems so fully documented as to need no further addition. But character is always fascinating, and through Mary Eleanor, Marjorie Campbell makes the past live for us again.

LOVAT DICKSON

Odyssey

I never remember her as middle-aged. She never looked like Whistler's venerable mother in the engraving father hung on the log wall of our first primitive Saskatchewan home. Nor have I thought of her as one of those ancient earth mothers who each in her successive generation founded a fecund, adapting people; yet she was one of them.

Instead, I remember her rehearsing a song, tea towel in hand, swaying to an imagined accompaniment as she glanced at the score propped against the kitchen window. While father used to read to us at bed time — too often it was Kingsley's precept-laden *Water Babies* when he, and we, would have preferred Kipling's thrilling *Jungle Books* or *Just So Stories* — she sang about a goldfish swimming in a big glass bowl and such lovely lullabies as "All Through the Night." She improvised games, on sunny days driving Nora and me around the lonely farmyard like a team of horses; when the weather was bad we raced halved walnut shells on a shallow milk pan of water, each tiny craft powered by a blazing sculpted Brazil-nut sail. As a special treat we played with the unlikely collection of treasures in her glove box — the crystal vial with the lingering scent of attar of roses, white kid gloves, a spent bullet that had saved father's life on one of his African safaris.

It was supper time when she died. Father had just started a new record on the gramophone, the lovely Bach Suite No. 3 in D Major, and sat down at the head of the table. Suddenly, he pushed back his chair and left us children alone. He stayed in her room until long after the music had ended, so long that I, at thirteen the eldest of her six little girls, though forbidden to touch it, carefully lifted the silent arm.

For us that supper hour marked the end of an era that I almost forgot in the aching realization that now we had no mother; in the disturbing changes that threatened to fill the void and in the anxious bewilderment of my younger sisters; throughout the exciting, growing-up years of adolescence and the late teens. I might actually have forgotten but for the persistent echo of the music that became its requiem.

That recording of Bach's haunting "Air on the G String" that half a century later sounds thin and scratchy was as moving to listeners newly accustomed to gramophones, even to a child, as the finest modern reproduction is to us today. Now, more than anything, merely to hear the first few bars of the "Air" evokes memories of my childhood before the First World War. Rather than calling back the heartache, it has made me aware of how little I really knew about the decade with which it ended, how blurred were scenes and even the face and voice of the woman who had filled our little world. Like an echo, the reminder persisted until I, a mature woman myself, longed to know more about her, to try to recapture something of her last years that must often have challenged her courage and love and endurance. And even if the "Air" and my natural curiosity had not prompted a search for her story, there was the pile of musical scores that eventually came into my care.

They were all worn, the corners of practically every number curled up where she had turned a page. Bach and Beethoven and Chopin. The entire score of the popular *Cloches de Corneville,* bound in black leather. Most well-known Gilbert and Sullivan works. Lovely ballads she had sung when she put Nora and me to bed or crooned as she nursed the latest baby. Operas and favorite music hall numbers. Here and there a jotted reference to Drury Lane or Covent Garden, or the name of an artist to indicate her love of the piano as well as her fondness for the songs and arias. But most poignant of all, the "Air" that I hope was the last sound she heard.

Though father seldom talked about her after that evening, he never failed to mention her on her birthday. Somehow he kept us all together, knowing that was what she would have wished above everything. It was what we all devoutly wished, too, and were grateful for as we grew to adulthood. Without one another we would have been utterly desolate, because the stresses of providing for us and filling in for a variety of domestic helpers often denied us his companionship. With it all he had no time for keeping in touch with mother's English relatives who never forgave him for taking her off to a land and a life they blamed for her untimely death. We never heard from them again.

Even father's relatives seemed impossibly remote as their letters dwindled to an annual Christmas event. With none of the usual bundles of family letters and carefully hoarded photos and mementoes and only father's hazily recalled recollections of the tragedy that had struck so long ago, more than once I would have abandoned the search but for those of her younger children who never really knew her.

Fortunately, other reminders gradually rose to the surface of my memory: father's farming records; letters from his younger brother, now living in New Zealand, who had sailed with him on a youthful trip to Cape Town; pioneers who had settled north of the Qu'Appelle Valley who might have something to tell me about her when I stirred their memories with the questions that were beginning to excite my every sortie into the story. Those early pioneer neighbors, the few I could expect to have survived in the area, could contribute much to the saga of men and women who succumbed, or rose splendidly, to the lure of the unknown frontier. Like my parents, they were all emigrants from somewhere. People who populate new worlds.

Though born in London, mother came from one of those enduring north country-border families. The Elliotts' use of the double *L* and the double *T* in their name had inspired such doggerel lines as "Who they be, no one can tell" and "Bastards be they and have since the sixteenth century"; they scarcely belonged to the famous Eliots.

No woman could have been less like the hackneyed ideal settler who allegedly originated with Canada's minister of agriculture, Clifford Sifton, the "man in the sheepskin coat with the big, broad wife." By comparison she was as small and deceptively fragile as a violet.

Canada, and particularly the vast unsettled spaces of Western Canada, next to Africa, was the last place in the world where she would have chosen to live. Father's descriptions of photographing and hunting big game in the diary he kept for her during three years in the Dark Continent after her early refusal to marry him had dismayed her as intensely as newspaper reports written by intrepid journalists who had sampled life in remote parts of the New World at the turn of the century. That dismay was something father never understood. He knew what he wanted to do and he assumed that what he wanted must be right, or at least best, for his wife and family.

They were as different as chalk and cheese, to use one of their favorite Edwardian metaphors. He was an arrogant young man, too full of that assumed superiority that made many an Englishman unpopular at the height of England's colonial supremacy; she belonged, heart and hearth, to London. He was a natural homesteader; without her piano and songs and music she was emotionally undernourished. Modern marriage counsellors would have warned against so unsuitable a match, but there were no marriage counsellors in their lives. If there had been they would never have listened to them. They were in love, and stayed in love as long as she lived, despite hardships neither could have imagined.

Immigrants

Around the turn of the century immigrants coming from densely populated old-world centers shared a common handicap: none of them could imagine the empty immensity of Western Canada. Only newcomers from the equally spacious Western United States accepted it more or less casually; Ontarians born on farms hacked out of hardwood forests had to realize that such apparently easy farming in no way guaranteed a quick and easy fortune.

Nor was that all. Because most of the already partially settled communities clustered close to the Canadian Pacific Railway that had been completed as late as 1885, every recently incorporated town and village tended to obscure the oceans of windswept grassland that had yet to feel the sharp cut of a ploughshare. Each man and his wife, if he was fortunate enough to escape the worst loneliness of a settler's initial years, whether European, American, or Eastern Canadian faced another staggering emotional hurdle. They had yet to feel the awful sense of isolation imposed by the unaccustomed space; that could affect their future as surely as their own efforts to meet the obvious priorities of survival. Fortunately, though the challenges of space and geography overwhelmed some of them, more grappled with themselves and the elements and won rewards beyond their most inspired dreams. They had found God's country.

It was the spring of 1904 when William Herbert Wilkins and his wife Mary Eleanor Elliott stepped from the colonist car at the little South Qu'Appelle railway station that, like every other station they had passed since leaving Winnipeg, had been painted deep *sang de boeuf*, the color of dried blood. He carried the baby and she held tightly to the two-year-old while the wind tugged at her hat and wrapped her skirt about her ankles.

As they paused on the plank platform with their piles of boxes and portmanteaux, not even a discerning observer would have imagined that as well as that inherent British arrogance, father also leaned strongly toward the Fabian socialism that had taken London by storm. He looked as though he belonged to his new surroundings. The Van Dyke beard currently popular in London complemented his assured walk; both confirmed his easy acceptance of an Englishman's privileged role in a still largely colonial world. The old felt hat, the best Johannesburg had been able to produce during his three-year stay in southern Africa, the Norfolk jacket, and the high leather boots merged well with the ugly red station building. A deep, appreciative gulp of clean, invigorating South Qu'Appelle air confirmed his every hope. It was "All Sir Garnet" as he used to say, recalling the African conquests of Sir Garnet Woolesley. And father liked to be right. He could not help the fact that his grasp sometimes failed to match his reach. Fortunately for us all, that day he had no inkling of the many occasions when merely to want to reach would be a distinct asset to him, as to every pioneer settler.

Naturally, he never quite realized how different it all looked to mother. Perhaps he never tried, knowing that she must eventually get used to their new way of life. He was not indifferent. He was merely facing fact, and every phase of the long train journey across Canada from Quebec had actually mattered more than the fact that until they sailed from Liverpool she had never been out of London except for brief holidays in Yorkshire or on the continent. Though for him the discomforts of the Immigration Hall at Winnipeg were no worse than many he had experienced in Africa, for her they were appalling. She had been horrified by the casual mingling of complete strangers in the much publicized Gateway to the Golden West that he had passed off with the assurance that they would soon be on their own place.

For her it had all been too swift and too overwhelming. She needed more than a few weeks and months to understand that the West cared little for old-world distinctions between a lady and a woman. Despite her acceptance of father's trust in her adaptability, she could not have helped the slightly disdainful swish of her long, modishly dust-ruffled skirt as she followed him along the plank sidewalk to their boarding house.

When I drove east from Regina on the search for my immigrant parents' story, twenty-five years after mother's death, my immediate goal was to try to recreate father's initial trek to inspect his farmsite. Only by sharing, or trying to share, the sixty miles he tramped could I begin to understand his hopes and his impelling dream. Merely to travel the modern paved highway that had replaced the dusty, deeply rutted trail of 1904 might help me to avoid perpetuating my own errors of memory and his. Seventeen miles north of South Qu'Appelle I drew over to the shoulder and switched off the ignition.

It was there that he must have felt his first moment of satisfaction in his choice of the general location of our new home. At the land office in Winnipeg where the Canadian government offered each aspiring settler a quarter section of free land he had studied the huge map indicating the character of soil in various areas of the North West Territories. Not for him the flat, bare prairie and potential square miles of wheat fields. He had set his heart on mixed farming such as he remembered from his schoolboy holidays in Yorkshire and the Vale of Aylesbury — well-treed land with a good supply of water and soil that would produce gardens and fodder as well as larger cash crops. For a token fee of ten dollars he had acquired 160 acres of semi-parkland on the eastern fringe of the open prairie described as Palliser's Triangle.

Seventeen miles north of South Qu'Appelle, where I parked and he had camped, he was still only a third of the way to the acres he longed to own, a longish walk even for a man who had trudged hundreds of miles south of the Zambezi River. Shedding his pack — a blanket and such essentials as bacon, salt, tea, and the billy for boiling water — he carefully collected dry twigs for his supper fire.

"I was reaching for my match, when I noticed, out of the corner of my eye, a slight movement. There, standing to get a good look at me, was my first meal of the trail, a rabbit. Reaching quietly for my gun, I gave him a formal invitation to join my pot of mulligan.

"Well fed and my blanket rolled about me, I could not sleep until I had filled my soul with the glory of the heavens. I had come five thousand miles and rejected the comfortable past for this life, and I revelled in its first taste."

Remembering that night, I understood as much as I could ever really understand what had brought him there. I recalled his vivid description of the fine country, the glorious spring night and the sky ablaze with stars. It was freedom in the truest sense of the word, he used to say, the experience that had made him question the virtue of life in a crowded, hampered city. Happily stretched out on the ground, he had "picked up the Pole star and one constellation after another and slowly dreamed down the Milky Way into sleep."

A location closer to transportation would have tempted any man less dedicated to pioneering, and with more capital. Father had little choice. That huge land map in the Winnipeg office had clearly indicated that practically all land near the railway belonged either to the C.P.R. and the Hudson's Bay Company or had been pre-empted by land companies determined to see it as the government brochures had advertised, "the land of golden opportunity." Instead of paying ten or twelve dollars an acre, he saved his modest capital to outfit his farm and provide for his family until the land produced the paying crops on which he counted. He also hoped that another quarter section next to his would still be available when he prospered and could afford to buy it.

A good night's sleep sweetened any lingering resentment he might have felt toward the land companies at the end of yesterday's long walk. As dawn unfolded the lovely panorama of the Qu'Appelle Valley below his campsite, the splendidly extravagant inducements offered Britons and Europeans by the Canadian government took on a more reasonable aspect. The promises of *Free Land* and *Homes for Millions* with which Canada lured settlers for its vast unpeopled spaces might have some validity after all. Father began to feel he was part of that *Last, Best West* he had read about so often in the London newspapers.

"With the lovely Qu'Appelle lakes as the immediate goal and the refreshing possibility of a swim, I was soon holding back with my pack as I almost rolled down the steep cut that leads into Fort Qu'Appelle, with the Anglican church steeple on the west side of the road and the flag of the Hudson's Bay Company on the right."

While father filled his brandy flask and paid for a package of the Hudson's Bay Company's best pipe tobacco, the elderly factor told him how the valley got its name.

Long ago, perhaps as much as two hundred years, so the legend ran by 1904, a young Indian brave sped his canoe across the lake to claim his promised bride. Suddenly, above the sound of the wind he distinctly heard his name. Resting his paddle, he listened. Then, "Who calls?" he cried in the French tongue he had learned from the Montreal fur traders who in their pack of trade goods had brought the traps that had changed the character of the Indians' major industry, but only his own voice mocked his sudden fear.

The death fires burning at her father's camp confirmed what he already knew: the dying maiden's last words had been for him. Silently he turned and strode to his canoe. He was never seen again, but to this day, said the factor, if you listen when the rising moon tops the valley, you can hear the lover's "Qui appelle?" that has become Qu'Appelle.

Father thanked him, adding that he expected they would meet again when he returned from inspecting his farmsite and brought his wife and children from South Qu'Appelle.

Mother never volunteered comments about the boarding house where she spent her first ten days in Canada while father trekked northward. It was he who later told me about it.

"The accommodation which I secured for my family while I went off reconnoitering was quite unlike anything they had ever experienced before. It was very rough and ready. Luxury was obviously absent, and the loneliness must have been almost as intolerable to a city-bred woman as the unknown fears of being alone in so enormous a country."

The boarding-house bedroom was so small they had to stow most of their luggage under the iron bedstead. There was literally no room for cots for the children, had there been any cots; when they appealed to their over-worked landlady, her solution was simple and practical.

"Most folks bed down their small kids in the dresser drawers."

Mother improvised our first Western Canadian beds by folding blankets for mattresses in the drawers father placed on a couple of trunks, joking about actresses at home who often resorted to similar arrangements while travelling in the provinces. They both welcomed the raucous supper bell that gave them an opportunity to escape from the crowded bedroom. Though mother, busy feeding her hungry children, scarcely entered into the conversation around the table, she marvelled at the ease with which father exchanged experiences with the other settlers and obtained so much valuable information from them about local conditions and weather.

Two days later when he left at dawn to inspect the quarter section, she watched him stride north along the rutted trail, scarcely able to recognize his sturdy figure in the unfamiliar breeches and high boots. She had never before seen him with a pack on his back and the double-barreled gun in the crook of his arm, except in the African albums. The very strangeness made her feel lonely. When, almost out of sight on the horizon, he turned and waved his hat, the loneliness overwhelmed her. Desolate as she had never been, she turned and rushed back to the boarding house and upstairs to the children who were just awakening.

Missing the rocking chair she had always sat in while nursing her babies, now she braced herself on the edge of the bed. When she had unbuttoned her blouse and cradled the infant against her breast she cuddled the toddler close in her other arm. She told herself that of course he would be back again in a week or ten days, as he had promised. Yet despite her every gallant effort she could not help thinking about what she would do if something happened to him, some accident she never allowed herself to formulate into any kind of reality. At the edges of her mind there lurked the terror familiar to every pioneer woman under similar circumstances in Western Canada, the fear bred of lurid newspaper stories about scalpings and other atrocities by savage Red Indians; the very fact that she knew nothing about native Canadians heightened every imagined scene.

During the rest of the long day, she left the bedroom only to take the children downstairs for meals. When they were in bed and asleep she faced the long night vigil and her own future.

First, she had to face up to her terrifying loneliness, not easy for a woman accustomed to city life and the close proximity of a warm group of family and friends. She longed for them all, but particularly for her sisters. Min, also recently married, had always been her loyal, staunch supporter even more than the gay, carefree younger Kate. In the ugly, cluttered bedroom, the mental picture of Kate seemed so preposterous that it forced a wry smile as mother thought of the many photos in their boxes and bales of settlers' effects — particularly the portrait of her younger sister in the long elegant gown with the slight sweeping train. I remember that photo well because as a child I quite naturally thought that so slender and beautiful a lady must be the queen.

Thoughts of the pleasant Highgate villa she had gone to as a bride evoked waves of nostalgia until she began to wonder if the pleasant suburb beside Hampstead Heath had actually existed; if the high, clear air that for centuries had attracted some of London's famous painters and writers was something she had read about. They had been so proud of the little drawing room where they arranged father's African trophies and the dining room with the sideboard he had made. In the dark she pictured the greenhouse where he grew his lilies; the darkroom under the stair where he developed photos; and the piano she had longed to bring with them. Why had they left it all for this raw, empty, lonely land?

Eventually she slept from sheer exhaustion and wakened to a wonderfully bright prairie dawn. In her lonely bed she tried to picture him somewhere, as alone as when she had watched him walk into the horizon, and she hoped that he, too, was enjoying the fresh, fragrant wind that billowed the cretonne curtain halfway across her bedroom. Suddenly she wanted him. She longed for him with an ardor she had never known, with a rush of emotion that made her realize, shyly even to herself, that she might become a very passionate woman if she ever again had the opportunity.

That early morning she wrestled with her fears and her emotions, "stood herself up in a corner" as her north country-lowland Scots ancestors would have said. The sight of her travelling costume hanging on a nail hammered into the wall reminded her of the day they had sat for their emigration photo. She had worn the costume that day, more conscious of the smart three-tiered long skirt and the long jacket than of the actual implications of the step they were taking. She had liked her Breton felt hat trimmed with the gay bird's wing and the high laced boots as much as she liked the capes and bonnets the children wore — fawn woollen material with matching fawn silk linings; the material for the capes and bonnets had been the same as the explorer Fridjof Nansen had chosen for his arctic expedition and so should be warm enough for Canada. She even remembered the hole in the baby's white sock and wished that I, her eldest, on father's knee had not been grizzling for dinner just when the camera clicked.

Struggling to overcome her nostalgia, she thought about him sitting for that photo in his fedora and tweeds, wearing the new gloves she had given him for his birthday. She had thought he was carrying his pioneer plans a bit too far when he packed the breeches and the old felt hat in their hand luggage instead of in one of the trunks. She herself had rejected his suggestion that she have something handy that would be comfortable to wear when they arrived at South Qu'Appelle.

A swift twinge of remorse quickly gave way to an overwhelming realization of how little she knew about what this venture meant to him. In London it had been natural and easy to understand the business life that was relatively familiar, even to a woman, and she had shared many an experience with him and listened to his accounts of people he met in the City. Everything about Canada had been beyond her comprehension. Lacking his years in Africa, she had nothing on which to base her imagination had she wished to try, and in her aversion to leaving home she had not consciously tried. Now she was in Canada, Western Canada, and the new life had commenced. Though she sensed that she was poor stuff for a settler's wife, for the first time she wanted to know what he might expect of her.

Quietly, so as not to waken the children, she got out of bed. At the narrow, oak-veneered washstand she poured cold water from the enameled iron jug and in the basin made her first attempt to wash away some of the worst handicaps of her incongruous past.

She knew she must keep herself busy, and so she got the children up and took them down to breakfast. Later, when the landlady showed her the washtub outside by the kitchen door and the scrub board hanging above it, she carried down the baby and a couple of the bulging bags of laundry that had accumulated since they left the boat. With the children beside her on a steamer rug on the wonderfully dry prairie grass, she actually enjoyed her chore and cheerily called out to the landlady for the wash boiler.

"We never boil diapers here," she was told. "We just hang 'em on the line and the wind does the bleaching." It was mother's first real lesson as a settler's wife.

For an entire week she tried not to look north along the trail that drew her eyes like a magnet. She made herself overcome her city dweller's aversion to meeting strangers and talked to the two other settlers' wives, each anxiously awaiting her husband's return. With them or alone, she spent hours pushing the baby's folding pram along the rough plank walk that ended in nothing at the edge of the town. After a few days she realized she could recognize the fresh pungeance of Balm of Gilead buds on the saplings in front of one of the unpainted frame houses. Her main disappointment that week was her inability to locate their own boxes among the huge piles of settlers' effects stacked in the railway station.

It was late on the evening of the seventh day when she heard father's voice and rushed downstairs to welcome him. She threw herself into his arms, sobbing in her relief and joy, oblivious to the other settlers in the room. When she did realize where she was, embarrassed by such a display of emotion in front of strangers, she tried to cover her confusion by dabbing at her eyes, standing back to get a better look at him in the lamp light.

Was this tanned, healthy-looking man really the one who had kissed her and trudged away into the north? While he ate his late supper she continued to marvel at his appearance and at his obvious satisfaction in his choice of the quarter section. Longing for details of their own place, she listened impatiently while he answered questions from the other deeply concerned immigrants. Hours later, it seemed, she ushered him up to the relative privacy of their bedroom where the children lay asleep.

That Edwardian gentlewoman brought up under the restraints of late Victorian middle class modesty would have been horrified if she knew that any of her daughters would think about how her parents spent that night in the lumpy bed in the strange boarding house with the cardboard-thin walls. She was by no means a frigid woman and in common with many women of her day she believed that because she was still nursing her baby she risked little possibility of becoming pregnant. They had spent six weeks in narrow beds in the close quarters of their tiny cabin aboard the C.P.R. S.S. *Bavarian,* on the colonist train, in the Immigration Hall at Winnipeg, and those two strange, fearsome first nights in the boarding house. Her husband had tramped and camped for a week out of doors, and alone. They were overwhelmingly ready for one another and the solace that made many a pioneer woman's isolation and hardships bearable.

Without that happy night together and despite her resolves, mother unhesitatingly would have refused to accept the shocking situation with which father confronted her the next morning when he led her out to inspect the equipage he had bought in Fort Qu'Appelle.

In the scraps of conversation since he returned, he had been delighted with the quarter section that was all he had hoped for. He had talked about the sloughs and the trees that dotted the prairie all the way north from the valley and how he had reached down to the roots of the long grass to pick violets that were as fine as any he had bought her at Covent Garden. To prove it he presented her with several, crushed and dry after days in his breast pocket but still showing their deep violet color. That grass would make first-class hay.

But nothing he had said prepared her for the shock of that equipage. She had expected to see a fine team of horses, and perhaps some sort of carriage. Never having imagined how they would move their belongings from the railway station to the new farm, she was utterly unprepared for father's solution. Their equipage — he obviously savored the term — was a high green wagon box on wheels. Hobbled nearby were two great, heavy oxen, beasts she had hitherto seen only in Dutch paintings at the galleries, or hauling drays.

"Sandy and Pat." Father introduced them proudly, his words tumbling out as he recited his experiences in the village in the valley. He had quickly declined a team of work-worn horses shipped west from Ontario for quick sale "to some greenhorn Englishman who could not size up a horse!" Relying on his African knowledge of oxen, he had bought the pair; had fitted them with bridles, bits, and yokes, and had actually broken them to harness on the way from the Fort. They had cost less than the old horses that would likely have collapsed before they reached the farm, and they would haul the loaded wagon as well as do the first season's ploughing.

He was so pleased with his purchase that he had not sensed her consternation, not until he turned from the oxen to face her for the approval he so obviously expected. Before she could think of suitably appreciative words, he made them impossible with his next statement: she and the children were to travel on the narrow seat on top of the load, when he had filled the wagon with their possessions stored in the railway station.

Again she was handicapped by her ignorance. She had never seen a woman riding on top of such an equipage, except, perhaps, a Breton fisherwife. Naively, she could not imagine herself in the role of a peasant. She did not know that every pioneer woman would ride to her new home as he had suggested. Nor did she understand that the high seat would be reasonably safe for herself and the children.

Choked by words she could not speak, tears flooding her eyes, she turned and rushed along the street to the boarding house.

How could he make so preposterous a suggestion, the man — her husband — who less than two years ago had accepted the freedom of the City of London at the memorable Guild Hall ceremony? Whose many amateur albums of highly professional photographs recorded the old queen's jubilee in Johannesburg and her London funeral followed by the new king's coronation, as well as so much African wildlife? The young man she had first seen coming down the stair at a friend's home, hat and neatly rolled gloves and cane in hand, and loved at first sight; the man their friends affectionately called the Duke? She remembered it all in a flash, and wondered how she could have agreed to marry him three years after their quarrel that had sent him off to Cape Town.

As surprised by her consternation as she was offended by his suggestion, not yet comprehending how little she could appreciate of the life to which he had brought her, father followed her to the small, overcrowded room where so recently they had made love. He found her already nursing the fretting baby, trying at the same time to dress the toddler.

She might have become hysterical and refused to accompany him under such conditions. She could have insisted on returning to England, selling her few pieces of jewelry to see her through until she could throw herself on the understanding sympathy of her relatives at home. Yet she knew, as most women of her generation knew full well, that she had no real alternative. In those early days of the twentieth century a wife did not lightly leave her husband no matter how bitterly they disagreed or how affronted she felt. Besides, she had two children and they were strangers in a strange country, completely without friends and almost without acquaintances.

She was ready to go with him when the wagon was packed. Their departure had been delayed for days because several crates of their possessions had been mislaid aboard the *Bavarian* en route to Quebec. They were never found nor was restitution ever made, not an uncommon experience that impoverished many a settler's home and further tested the brave spirits of the most gallant women. Even without the missing crates, the high wagon box was overloaded for the early morning start.

Mother wore the only travelling costume she had until their boxes could be unpacked. Father held the baby while she grasped the long skirt and struggled up onto the high seat. Then he handed up the baby and lifted the toddler to a place beside her. There was nothing he could do, had he tried, to help her with the hat that threatened to escape its long pins and sail off in the strong, gusty wind.

Without his brief account of that departure I would never have believed it happened.

"No amount of imagination could quite picture the sheer lunacy of that trip. The only excuse is that most explorers and pioneers are considered fools by the sane of their community. Friends and relatives in England would have sought means of preventing such foolhardiness.

"A green Englishman with most of his goods and chattels piled high on a wagon, and, hitched to the clumsy vehicle, a pair of green oxen. The crowning bit of folly was the slim, steady-eyed young woman, attired in her London-made costume, seated with her two children on top of the nearly top-heavy load."

The cheering citizens of South Qu'Appelle wished them good luck. Father gripped the rhinoceros-hide *sjambok* that was one of his prized African souvenirs, gaily waving the whip in farewell. He flicked the near ox, and the Wilkins family headed north.

Like the boarding-house experience, mother seldom talked about that journey. From the top of the high load the vast countryside looked utterly empty, the horizon endless. The slow, steady swaying of the oxen's broad backs made her feel giddy. Struggling to keep her balance and to hold the two children, she tried to remind herself that they were on the last lap of their journey to the new home, hoping it might resemble the few farmhouses they had passed near South Qu'Appelle and that it would be near enough for her to have a dog cart to drive in for shopping. But no amount of dreaming could relieve her growing tension.

By the time father suggested a rest she nearly fell into his arms. Mercifully, she never knew of his later biographical comment that the load was heavy and the oxen not yet fully broken to their yokes.

They made a much longer stop for lunch at the spot where I parked the car, overlooking the lovely wide valley that, despite its village, in no way resembled an old-world community long lived in by generations of families.

While father unpacked their bread and cheese and cold tea, mother fed and changed the baby and found a level spot in the long grass for the toddler's white enamel potty. When she had tended to their needs she turned to father in sudden consternation.

"What shall I do for a W.C.?"

"What the native women do, I suppose," he suggested practically.

"Or the gypsies!" she retorted, trying to accept the situation. Lifting her long skirts in the long grass behind the wagon, she learned how desperately she needed to accomplish what she later saw Indians performing easily and naturally as women have done since the beginning of the species.

From my vantage point on a seat of the rented car I tried to imagine father's dilemma as he surveyed the rutted trail that meandered down the long coulee to Fort Qu'Appelle. Trekkers approaching a steep river bed in Africa had had at least one helper to lead the oxen or mules while the driver sought the safest means of descending the steep grade. He was alone, except for mother and the children, and not even when he had suggested that she ride on that high seat, the suggestion that had so shocked her sense of propriety and safety, had he considered risking their lives on that treacherous slope.

But she was learning; she had sized up the situation and decided to follow as close as she could. The ordeal was a nightmare for both of them, recalled by him in a wry sort of triumph.

"A logging chain wrapped about one of the wheel fellows acted as a partially effective brake, and from the top of the load I endeavoured to hold the steers in check, driving them from side to side on the trail to lessen the slope."

No African trekker ever sweated more than father did as he cajoled and coerced the ponderous beasts from side to side to ease the gradient, knowing that a lurch of the heavy load could not only crush them but jeopardize the entire venture. Flicking the near ox's flank with the sjambok, he alternated gentle persuasion with loud Swahili words, too intently involved to give a thought to his wife struggling behind, falling and picking up herself and the children as she stumbled over the ruts.

The descent took as long as the entire journey from South Qu'Appelle, with many pauses to rest the oxen. At the last pause, he called back to her: "See that flat stretch near the bottom of the slope?" He indicated it with the whip. "That's where you ride again — into town in style!"

For a moment his absurd suggestion of riding into the Fort in style broke the tension, though only her fatigue forced her to climb back on to the high seat.

"We created a mild furore when we unhitched at the fort," he recalled. But the mild furore was not due to the appearance of a well-dressed woman and two children on top of the load, such bizarre scenes were becoming familiar as new settlers paused at Fort Qu'Appelle in their journey to potential farms. No one had expected to see father return with the green oxen he had purchased only a week before, least of all the harness maker who had fitted the oxen with bridles, bits, and yoke, who "would never have sat up there with them green bulls for anything."

Mother would gladly have settled as near as possible to the village that, despite its relative newness, reminded her of England more than anything she had seen in Canada — the quality that inspired the Scottish painter James Henderson a few years later to make it his home and the subject of several fine canvases. The little church and the Hudson's Bay Company store, the primitive houses that looked lived in answered a longing that daily had increased since they stepped onto the railway platform at South Qu'Appelle.

Father had other ideas.

Instead of staying at the local hotel, he insisted on camping beside Echo Lake; the sooner she got used to pioneer ways, the sooner mother would learn to enjoy the life.

On his way north he had selected a dry campsite for their first night on the journey and there, after unloading bedrolls and overnight needs, he pitched their bell tent.

"I expect you'd like a cup of tea," he said as he made a neat little fire, filled the billy from the lake, and set it on his improvised tripod to boil.

They spent the night on a couple of blankets on an oilcloth ground cover spread out in the tent. Bone weary from his strenuous day, father slept the moment his head touched the folded jacket that was his pillow. Both children slept well too. Only mother remained awake, listening to the strange sounds that filled her little world: the ripple of water on the lake; winds blowing down the coulee and along the valley; a restless bird; dogs barking in the distance; ominous choruses of frogs. She prayed that no wild animal would break into the tent and that the oxen would not escape their hobbles. Never had she felt lonelier, not even during her first night alone at the boarding house. Yet she might have felt almost happy had she known how much father appreciated her contribution to their first day on the trail.

"Men alone," he recalled from the distance of several years, "can easily find three meals a day and a bed in which to sleep. But that is all. It takes a woman to make living quarters, even though very temporary and in nothing more than a head-lowering, back-bending bell tent."

In spite of her terrors and apprehensions she eventually slept until he wakened her with the announcement that breakfast was ready — porridge for the children, tea and ember-grilled fish for themselves. Though she would have preferred to have the fish cooked in the frying pan, she had to admit that it was delicious and gladly delayed their departure while he enjoyed a little fishing.

"Of course I was determined that we should be as self-sufficient as possible, and I had caught a fine pike on my first trip. This time, instead of relying on a primitive hook and line I used the excellent tackle I had bought in London."

There is no doubt that father also enjoyed the prospect of showing the village boy who was casting nearby how fish should really be caught. To his disappointment, half an hour later he had not had a single bite and the boy had packed up and left with all he could carry.

"My cup was about full when my wife began to make suggestions. As she had never fished even for tiddlers or crawfish, I might be pardoned for not receiving her suggestions in the best of grace. Then, to add insult to injury, without the slightest hint of sadism she had hunted out the line and spoon which I had used on the earlier trip and, unknown to me, had dangled the spoon in the water. Suddenly there was an excited little scream. She had a fish all right, and because she did not like wiggley things, I landed the 4½ pound pike.

"My mortification was so deep that it led me to the conclusion that these fish were not yet educated to civilized ideas of fishing!"

But they had a long journey ahead, and shopping to do at the Fort for the provisions on mother's long list: sugar, flour, bacon, rolled oats, salt, canned milk, coffee beans, and tea. The tea came in one of the five-pound tin cannisters decorated with a colored picture of the old queen, a future collector's item and for years our handy cookie jar. Mother also bought a good supply of soap, and borax and lye, as well as a clothesline and clothespins. By the time her list was completed and the supplies had been loaded in the wagon she had almost mastered the Canadian money that had so greatly puzzled her in Winnipeg. Their departure was further delayed while father made enquiries about the trail and the condition of the bridge across the Narrows between Echo and Lebret lakes. News that the approach was under several feet of water demanded special advice but in no way deterred him, though it greatly alarmed mother. His main concern as he commanded the oxen to "Giddap!" was that the sun was already high in the sky and the day half-spent.

At the approach he hailed a man in a democrat who had reined in his team of horses while he surveyed the situation. The stranger, a rancher anxious to get to his own place westward along the valley rim before dark, agreed that the crossing was risky but not impossible. They would have to take the approach carefully, and he offered to drive mother and us children across, leaving father free to give his full attention to managing the oxen and the heavy load.

Both men ignored her anxious attempt to delay the departure that to her threatened our very lives. While the rancher jumped down from the democrat and helped her up to the high seat, father held the baby and then handed the toddler up to a snug place between them. The rancher in his wide sombrero and high-heel boots gripped the reins firmly, spoke quietly to his team and they lunged into the murky, deep, swirling water. Terrified as she clutched the baby with one arm and held the toddler with the other, mother saw it rise to the nearest hub. The turning wheels churned the water like the wash of a fast boat until it sprayed her face. Without knowing what she did, or why, she braced her feet against the dash board. Moments later, when the horses' hooves clattered onto the firm surface of the bridge, she knew she had been so intent on sharing the ordeal that she had forgotten all trace of her personal fear. As the wheels rattled over the gravel at the far side of the Narrows she casually ignored the muddy water that dripped from the sopping wet hem of her dust-ruffled skirt and her boots.

"With her heart in her mouth," tense and very quiet beside her benefactor, she watched father reach for the oxen's bridles. His boots tied to their laces and hanging about his neck, trousers rolled to his knees, he led the beasts forward — another pioneer legend was about to be born. In his own words:

"The swirl of the water was useful. It served to show where the embankment dropped away some twelve feet on either side of the inundated road.

"The look of relief on your mother's face when I finally made it I shall never forget. Myself, I had no time to think about anything but keeping the wagon on that approach I could not see. A foot too far on either side and the wagon loaded with everything we needed would have toppled into ten or twelve feet of water, to say nothing of the oxen on which we depended, and even myself!"

The rancher congratulated father warmly; he himself would never have risked it with his wife and a couple of children. Before driving away, he took a long look up the telegraph hill coulee, father's next challenge, and wished him good luck. Father welcomed the good wishes.

"I had feared the 350 foot climb from the valley more than crossing the Narrows. Our team could not possibly make a continuous trip up to the level of the prairie, so steep was the climb."

At the Fort he had bought several heavy timbers, hanging them under the wagon for use when he would have to scotch the wheels as he gave the oxen much needed rests. Unlike the descent, this time he had the added worry of his family: mother could not possibly carry two children up that long, steep trail, at least as rough and rutted as the descent on the other side of the valley.

Those few days at the beginning of their actual pioneering journey may have reminded him of the difference in their outlook and experience. He even sensed something of her silent terror as she crouched on her high seat and watched him lead his oxen from one side of the trail to the other to lessen the gradient; several times pausing to secure the rear wheels with the timbers, he glanced up at her with a reassuring wave of the sjambok.

The oxen were surefooted and now accustomed to his firm commands. They responded well to the occasional African epithets she chose not to understand; she knew those weird words bolstered his determination to meet this as well as every other challenge of the journey. When the valley lay far below and the prairie stretched flat and northward ahead of them, she understood his exultant words:

"The youth who cried 'Excelsior' was no more overjoyed than we to reach the summit."

He pitched the tent while she unpacked the supper basket. It was the family's first night alone on the prairies. Last night they had been within less than a mile of Fort Qu'Appelle and all the usual, usually muffled after-dark sounds of two or three hundred people. Across the Narrows, as dusk fell, the coulees echoed the deep-throated voices of the Oblate Fathers at Lebret as they chanted their vespers, and the high, thin voices of Indian children at one of the earliest residential Indian schools in the West. Incredulous, and awed by what they must have felt to be some sort of omen, father and mother had listened to the *"Kyrie Eleison"* that reminded them poignantly of the summer Sunday a few months after they were married when they visited Ely Cathedral and father had made the photo of the choristers chanting the ancient "Lord Have Mercy Upon Us." They had brought the photo with them, a souvenir of the former home that was to become part of the new.

Tonight they heard no vespers; no sounds from the village reminded them that other men and women and children lived in this new land. Long before dark their own children slept on their improvised beds on the ground. And as dusk settled the stars began to shine, larger and more luminous than any mother had ever seen, accustomed as she had been to the gas lights that dimmed London's night-time skies if the fog did not. A palpable stillness surrounded their tent, and a silence that was disturbed only by a strange, distant sound that seemed as though it could be felt.

They had settled down on their blankets when father got up to see what was making the oxen restless and to check their hobbles. She could see him silhouetted against the open tent flap, listening, in no way troubled by the vague apprehension his questioning stance evoked in her. Suddenly, he called quietly to her: she must get up and come out to see what might be her first real introduction to prairie life.

"Over there!" he said, taking her arm and directing her to what looked like a dark, stirring cloud against the horizon. She could actually feel the sound, a strange monotonous thudding that made her think of an earthquake. What she could see and hear, father told her in his quietly excited voice, was a huge herd of cattle, hundreds of hooves held together by the equally monotonous singing of several cowboys, who, in turn, would ride around them all through the night. Fifty years ago, instead of cattle, such a herd would have been wild buffalo.

As they slowly approached, one of the cowboys warned them not to come too close or to make a sudden noise that might cause the herd to stampede.

Back in their tent and with their ears close to the ground, as they listened the settlers realized that the thudding hooves had quietened to the steady murmuring of tired animals contentedly chewing their cuds and that weird, endless accompaniment of low-pitched cowboy songs. Soon, they, too, slept.

The sound and the renewed feeling of thudding hooves wakened them at dawn. From the open tent, they watched the herd move toward the valley shoulder like a dark cloud shadow that slowly disappeared on its way to the valley and the river crossing. At the last glimpse, father warned mother that she must not be carried away by romantic ideas about huge ranches; here the ranchers, as had sometimes occurred in Africa, threatened the existence of every potential farmer.

The sight of the herd moving toward South Qu'Appelle and the railway reminded them sharply that they still had a long journey ahead, in the opposite direction. But before they set off, while mother packed the breakfast things, father took his gun and soon bagged a couple of ducks feeding near a large slough and in his hat brought back half a dozen eggs, "for a supper omelet." The lovely warm day was still merely a promise when mother took her last, longing look in the direction of the comfortable village in the valley and settled herself and us children on the high seat.

The Touchwood Trail, several tracks wide, followed the telegraph poles that had been a familiar sight to Hudson's Bay Company carters since the Northwest Rebellion of 1885, linking Prince Albert on the North Saskatchewan River to the railway at South Qu'Appelle. Some of those trains of ox carts, hauling supplies to northern trappers or returning with baled furs, stopped overnight at the only halfway accommodation between the valley and the farmsite. Father merely waved a greeting to the Métis settler, Sangré, who offered travellers a bed on his unwashed kitchen floor and breakfast of tea and porridge at fifty cents a person. Having paid the necessary courtesy to a fellow settler, he knew mother would prefer the privacy of their tent. He stopped instead at the next sod-roofed shack, where to mother's surprise a man whom she mistook for a typical old-country laborer welcomed her gallantly.

"We'll be neighbors," he said after the introductions. "I expect to see a town spring up right here on my acres when the new railway branch comes along. Make my fortune here. You won't know this country in a few years," he assured mother so confidently that for a moment she had to believe him, despite the complete absence of any other sign of habitation on the vast empty horizon.

Father easily shared this optimism. The men chatted about prairie opportunities and conditions on the trail and then they shook hands, and he wished us good luck.

"Let me know if there is anything I can do to help," he offered, waving his cap in farewell.

That night the immigrants camped on a pleasant little rise near a large slough where father dipped water for tea and the children's porridge. In the morning, and again it was a beautiful day, he carried more water for mother to wash the diapers she then spread to dry on the load behind her seat. As he rolled the bedding and the tent, he whistled and warbled snatches of song.

"We'll be home tomorrow," he assured her cheerily.

But the trail had become increasingly muddy from recent rains. Occasionally a deep bog forced him to steer the oxen through the long grass. After several such diversions the steers stopped at a long, deep water-filled hole, stolidly planting their hooves in the soft, yielding mud. When no amount of Swahili or flicks of the sjambok would move them, father accepted the obvious fact learned from long experience of observing African trekkers: no amount of flogging would move a tired animal.

The sky that had been clear and bright when they started out was now dark with cloud. With the first rain drops he informed mother that they were probably stuck for the rest of the day and night. Had the yoke been fresh, hours of backache and frustration might have been averted.

"There were my wife and children perched high on top of the load, but before rescuing them, the steers had to be unhitched. Then came the difficult problem of unloading, first the passengers, and then every parcel and bale in the load. Dry spots were at a premium, so it was a matter of selecting the least wet for a campsite. When it started to rain all sense of adventure left the situation. It was a frantic race with the elements, that unloading of the tent and camp utensils and food, and pitching the tent. The elements won, of course, but only partially. Soon the tent was up, a bit of a fire going and the promise of a hot drink relieved the moment of its gloomiest aspect.

"It was a miserable night. Never should we forget that one must never touch the sides of a tent during a rain storm. But it was all but impossible to avoid touching the canvas sides of that small bell tent.

"Morning is traditionally a time for seeing things in a better light. But to face that wagon, low in a pool of water, and knowing that the ground was soaked everywhere for miles, and that every article would have to be moved before the wagon could be rescued from the terrific suction of the mud, was not the cheeriest of prospects." That day even father would have given up pioneering.

It took him the entire morning to carry everything to firm ground, wading through mud and water with each load. When at last the wagon was empty he rehitched the rested oxen to the sturdy logging chain that had served so well on the descent to the valley. At his loud, desperate "Giddap" with an equally loud squelching sound the wagon slithered out of the mud at the first try.

While he spent the remainder of the day reloading the wagon, mother tried to keep us children amused, and, determined to help him instead of being the burden she had felt herself to be, prepared her first Canadian meal on the camp stove, "the most welcome meal" father ever ate. Another dawn brought another bright, warming, and drying sun and with his renewed optimism he promised her that "with luck, we will be home by noon!"

He had been leading the oxen ever since they left South Qu'Appelle, the sjambok over his shoulder like a musket, steadily trudging towards their elusive goal. From her high perch, hour after hour, mother had searched the horizon for another settler's shack or another stable that might suggest that they were getting near some sign of civilization. Though she tried not to look at the little garnet-rimmed watch pinned on her blouse, her eyes involuntarily sought it as a relief from so much space, the countless sloughs and poplar bluffs, the ocean of grass, and the rutted Touchwood Trail that threatened to go on to the very end of the world.

It seemed a week since they had passed the settler's shack, the home of their nearest neighbor, ten miles away. Or was it twice ten miles? Only father's occasional comments, tossed back over his shoulder as he guided the oxen, kept her from dozing on the seat and losing her firm grasp of the restless teething baby and her squirming toddler. She had long ago taken off our warm capes and bonnets and her own jacket. The high collar of her blouse was so soaked with perspiration that she thought it would choke her.

Though he had seemed to be oblivious to her discomfort during the journey so far, now he began to point out a specially large bluff and, again, a slough where at sunrise and sundown great flocks of ducks would find shelter and food; a badger's hole that might throw an unwary horseman. He recalled the high, sweet song of a meadow lark that had greeted them the morning they left the valley and that would again herald the dawn. Instead of the exhaustion mother could have understood, with every slow, plodding step some fresh source of energy quickened his gait and his enthusiasm. She marvelled at his stamina that seemed to match that of the oxen to whom he talked almost as though they were people.

It was not yet midday by her watch when he led them away from the rutted trail and its endless blanket stitching of telegraph poles. The sun burned her back and shoulders, and she longed for a parasol to protect herself and the children from its heat. Her arms ached from the weight of the heavy, whimpering baby. Too weary to regard it as more than a casual repetition of the gesture that usually signalled a stop, she saw father push back his hat. She could see no reason for a stop, and it was still too early for lunch. There was no house, no stable, nothing. To her amazement he halted the oxen, and his "Whoa, there" sounded like a paean of satisfaction and thanksgiving.

We were home.

Year One

No typical lady of the day would lightly accept a long wearying journey behind a yoke of oxen that ended without a semblance of a house or an excuse for the omission, certainly not mother. Struggling to hold back the tears of fatigue and bewildered disappointment, she asked the simple, halting question that every pioneer woman under similar circumstances has asked.

"Is — is this it?"

"This is it. Welcome home! Down you get. . . ."

But she did not move. Still struggling for words, almost in a whisper, she asked the next obvious question: How did he know this was home?

Again, as he had done at her immediate lack of approval for the equipage, he faced her, amazed at the dismay she could not disguise. This was the moment he had planned for for so long, the achievement that was all he had hoped for. Eager for her approval, anxious to reassure her, he reached into his vest pocket for his compass and the document stamped by the Department of Immigration, and he compared the two.

"North-west quarter Section 12, Township 25, Range 14, West 2nd Longtitude. . . ."

Had she not noticed the surveyor's four holes and the marker?

She had not, and if she had recognized the marker she would not then have realized that it constituted the sole means by which a settler identified the acres he had chosen or been alloted by the immigration authorities.

Out of the mass of typical pioneer homecomings, each settler came to cherish his own peculiar memories, the little events that colored that memorable day; like a wedding night, joyous or tragic, it could never happen again. Of the scores of such occasions remembered by scores of old-timers, one scene remains clear in my imagination: the man looking up from beside the loaded wagon, the woman cradling their children and trying to control her emotions as she looked down to him.

In their particular moment he must have recalled her spirited opposition to his suggestion that they emigrate to one of the colonies and the scene that triggered their first quarrel. She as vividly recalled his equally spirited retort that if she felt that way about it he would go to Africa alone, neither of them believing that he actually would book passage to Cape Town.

Under the hot noonday sun, marooned on this sea of grass, as she contrasted his eloquent descriptions of life in Canada with the reality, mother wished she had refused the pearl engagement ring and later the wedding ring he had brought her from Africa. Father, content with every promising aspect of his quarter section, in that long assessing moment wondered why he had written the fulsome diary addressed to *My Dearest Nellie* and now faced the possibility of having to transform 160 acres into a productive, prosperous farm with so seemingly hostile a wife.

Whatever their secret thoughts, there was no escape for either of them. No primitive boarding house where mother could now seek brief sanctuary. No accustomed farmyard chores to relieve father's amazed disappointment. Without the buffer companionship of relatives or friends and the solace of a sympathetic ear, they had to face the imperative need to evolve some sort of life together. No one would suggest separation or divorce or legal advice because there was no one within several days' journey.

Like every couple on every isolated pioneer farmsite they faced the long moments of agonizing letdown that followed actual arrival. Chained together by circumstances now beyond their immediate control, their only hope depended on sufficient intelligence and courtesy to make their life together bearable for one another and their children until neighbors began to arrive.

Father returned the compass to its little leather pouch and his pocket. He reached for us children and helped mother down from her inconveniently high seat, steadying her politely while she stretched her cramped, tense legs. When between them they knocked off her hat, he stooped for it and tossed it to the top of the load.

"You won't get sunstroke without a hat for a few minutes," he said, leading the way up the knoll with Nora in his arms. "Come and see the view for yourself."

She followed, one hand grasping me, the other trying to manage her skirt that impeded every step through grass as long as unmowed hay.

"You couldn't find a better site in all the Territories," father exulted, tactfully ignoring her difficulties. "Look in any direction, all across our place. Trees! Water! Land! What more could we ask for?"

It was futile to tell him that she longed for a house with beds and a kitchen and a sitting room where she could put the treasures and necessities piled on the wagon, so obviously had he forgotten everything but his satisfaction with what to her was less than nothing. On his earlier visit he had cut poplar stakes and laid out the boundaries for their house; now he showed her where they would put the front door so that she could look out across their acres. But she could not see what he saw. She could not match his enthusiasm. She could not picture the garden he planned to plough near the large slough that promised a good supply of water.

Father would have exulted over his splendid plans indefinitely but for the two hungry children, howling for their dinner. They changed the scene swiftly and dramatically. Minutes later mother nursed her baby, propped against a portmanteau on the grass. Father unloaded the tent and pitched it in front of the house site and the view she would learn to love and to hate. Then, while she opened the food hamper, he secured the tent pegs against the stiff wind and spread the oilcloth ground cover and the rug on which we all would sleep for months. He set up the folding camp table and the two folding chairs while she put the billy to boil on the camp stove, hoping that by the next meal they would have unpacked a real kettle.

They were both grateful for the primitive, essential tasks that kept conversation at bay. When the children were asleep and they at last sat down for their first meal on what father at least thought of as the site of their new house, he raised his camping mug with a restrained "Welcome Home!" Appreciating his courtesy, she raised her own mug with a grateful gesture. Despite their still tense attitudes, she felt relieved that she need not again climb aboard the hated wagon. As the wind blew a wisp of hair about her face she even welcomed the pungent fragrance of the Balm of Gilead she could now recognize. Only time and circumstances would enable her to decide whether the wind would be her benison or a curse.

That day not even father had time to reflect that the 160 acres would not legally be his for three years, not until he had made the improvements required under the terms of the Canada Land Act: he would have to erect a house and stable and plough the fields to prove his eligibility as a settler.

When they had eaten their first supper in front of the tent and the lingering dusk could no longer delay the moment they had both secretly dreaded, he spread their blankets. Again, they had no choice. No matter what their unspoken differences, they had to sleep together on the narrow space between the pole that supported the tent and the tent's low canvas wall.

Try as they might, neither could turn without touching the other, the touches that even on that first strange night beside the lake had delighted and excited them. Yet now, though each had anticipated an impossibly restless night, the fatigues of the journey and the wonderfully fresh air mercifully decided otherwise. They both slept minutes after their heads touched the pillow he had rummaged from the wagon. When they wakened hours later, refreshed emotionally and physically, they instinctively turned to one another.

They laughed at the incongruity of trying to make love on the ground, muffling their laughter so as not to waken the children asleep within reach on the other side of the pole, knowing that the slightest pressure against the prop would bring the tent down on them all and all it contained. Hours later they wakened again to their new day emotionally stronger and more adapting than when father had halted the oxen with his thankful "Whoa!"

Not even an Edwardian lady could continue to nurse her principles and cherish her genteel upbringing after lying on the ground beside the man she loved. Nor remain aloof. Sixty miles from the nearest railway station, on a quarter section of virgin Western Canadian prairie, having expressed her feelings clearly, she hoped, mother determined to try to make the best of their situation. But, inevitably, the unspoken, unanswered questions continued to nag at the back of her mind.

Had he known that their land would lack all improvements, or that the C.P.R., the Hudson's Bay and the speculating land companies already controlled practically every acre of land within easy access of transportation and markets? Had he realized that every enticing brochure omitted to inform potential settlers that they might have to live their early years several days distant from a post office, a doctor, or even a store where provisions could be replenished and household necessities purchased; that no one had thought to explain to a potential settler's wife the difficulties involved in living in a small bell tent with no facilities for storing even everyday clothing, without a shelf for crockery and cooking utensils, or a table on which to prepare the food stowed in an English copper boiler and a couple of inadequate packing cases? Was every pioneering woman expected to get along without an iron, and would the children's clothes never again resemble those she had proudly dressed them in at home? Had no one been responsible for attracting the kind of couples who would create an enduring sort of life in an empty land?

Often on my search for their pioneering story, I wished that some of mother's letters had survived. Lacking them, I had to rely almost entirely on father's version of all that had occurred and particularly for her reactions. Yet one thing I know, being her daughter and having inherited a little of her insight, no matter how many letters she wrote to her sisters and friends in London she would never have mentioned, not even to Min and Kate, her stunned emotions when father had halted the oxen beside the knoll. She would never have admitted to them that her husband, the man they had liked but felt would never settle down, had taken her so far from home without providing a house for her to live in. Above all, her sense of delicacy would have prevented her from describing their first achievement.

It was not the house she needed most that day when they arrived at the virgin site, it was a W.C. Despite six days on the trail from South Qu'Appelle she had not perfected her squatting stance nor learned to manage her long skirts in the grass.

They had no lumber; that would come later on trips to the Fort when father commenced work on the house. But he had his well-filled tool box, and there was an abundance of poplar in the bluff behind the knoll, the windbreak of his planned farmstead. Acutely aware that this delicate situation could seriously affect their future, he chopped down several sturdy poplars and erected a primitive little shelter, fashioning a comfortable seat from the boards he pried off the packing case that held the heavy, oak-framed engraving of Whistler's *Carlyle*. Though a lumber privy replaced the first necessity a couple of years later, the term W.C. lingered for years without running water. Buoyed by the continuing glorious weather, at the time they failed to appreciate how bizarre the stark little convenience looked, the sole evidence of human habitation from horizon to horizon, other than the tent and the oxen hobbled near the still-loaded wagon.

After the extreme exertions of the journey, for a couple of days they rested and explored the bluffs and sloughs close to the knoll. They discovered familiar plant life, particularly flowers, and strange clumps of pale grey shrub that resembled nothing they knew — the velvet leaves of wolf willow that in a few weeks sprouted tiny, unbelievably fragrant yellow flowers. They listened to the joyous early matins of the prairie lark as it soared out of sight in the blue sky that was never entirely free of restless white clouds. They might have prolonged their brief explorations but for the sudden, shocking discovery that they had underestimated the supply of condensed milk they had brought for the children.

Nothing could have reminded them more forcefully of how remote they were from everyday necessities to which they were accustomed. In the simple equation of pioneering, mother was weaning the baby and they had not seen a cow since leaving the valley.

Had they been respectful of prayer, and I know they were in their unorthodox way, the event that occurred the next morning would have served as an omen of divine approval of their undertaking, while at the same time confirming father's belief in a Divine Providence. At first they thought it must be a mirage or a miracle, that vision of a man walking toward their little camp from the east.

John Locktie introduced himself. A Scot who had filed on his quarter section the previous autumn, he had built his shack and a rude shelter for his animals and with them had survived the cold, lonely winter, spending most of the coldest days in his bed pushing a length of firewood into the heater on which he did his meagre cooking. He had heard father's rhythmic axe strokes and could hardly believe his ears. His cow had recently calved and, with apologies to mother and a courtly bow, he explained that he did not know how to milk a cow and he would be damned if he was going to learn. He hoped that his new neighbor possessed more knowledge and farming experience than he; in short, could father milk a cow and if he could, would he care to?

There were few things that father could not do, and one of our earliest memories was mother's amazement at his versatility. Faced with the necessity of finding milk for his children or wasting ten or twelve days going to the Fort for a supply, he gladly milked Locktie's cow for weeks, daily carrying his pail to the shack they could not see beyond its sheltering poplar bluff. Pleased with the quality of the milk, he eventually persuaded his first Canadian friend to sell him the precious animal.

Father and mother were only slightly less surprised when a second man appeared a few days later by way of the track leading in from the Touchwood Trail, a lean, lithe, elderly Indian called Old Antelope.

Trudging the two miles to Locktie's shack day after day had given father time to think seriously about his priorities; with plenty of milk, none now loomed as urgently as a well. The slough he had counted on to provide a convenient supply of water was already becoming brackish as the sun evaporated the shallow water. Through some well developed native grapevine, the Indian had heard of the new settler's arrival. For a dollar, he said, producing a forked stick from his handsomely beaded belt, he would find water. Father accepted the offer.

"Head down, holding the bent twig well out from his body with both hands, the old Indian walked back and forth across the farmsite. I saw the twig incline, whether occultly or not, and the Indian grunted."

Father paid him his dollar and a generous smoke of tobacco, the highly appreciated currency he had often depended on in Africa. Then he commenced digging on one of the sites he had already chosen. That first well "cribbed with saplings and later with lumber, provided us with water as long as we remained on the farm."

It also provided mother with her first and only experience at hard labor; while father dug she hauled up the pails of earth, heavier and heavier as the well deepened. She hated it. Her back ached. Her hands became sore and calloused. But someone had to help him, and there was no one except herself. When he struck water and had completed the cribbing, she insisted that he make some sort of covering for the children's protection, and he devised not only the top, from poplars, but also a convenient, well-secured opening through which they could lower perishable foods, the milk and canned butter and a side of bacon. It was the only relatively cool spot under the burning prairie sun.

Then he turned to the ploughing that gave him his first feeling of real achievement, the tiny garden plot.

Those few furrows, not as straight as he would have liked, were symbolic. They represented a beginning of the remote fruition of his dreams. For them he had travelled thousands of miles and uprooted his family. Now, a typically lone figure, the oxen's lines about his shoulders, his hands gripping the simple, single-share plough, he gloried in the prospect of mastering the virgin land.

But he was a practical dreamer. The furrows that looked as incongruous as the W.C. and whetted his longing for more, reminded him of his urgent need for the disc and harrows he had purchased at the Fort but had had to leave behind because there was no room for them on the loaded wagon. The oxen must have hay if they were to keep in condition to do the heavy work of ploughing the tough prairie sod. Instead of turning them out to forage for themselves he must also have a hay mower and rake, and the need inevitably evoked visions of several tidy stacks of well-cured hay. It all became logical and right but for the realization that he could not leave mother and us children alone for a couple of weeks.

The arrival of his younger brother Lionel became yet another fortunate coincidence that solved yet another pressing problem.

They had known before leaving London that Leo planned to retire from the Royal Navy on completion of his training in the Far East. After spending a few weeks in England, he had decided to try farming in Western Canada, lured as father had been by those tempting offers of free land; though his quarter section was a mile away to the east, he immediately decided to pitch his tent near his older brother.

When the driver of the democrat he had hired at South Qu'Appelle waved good-bye, he announced that he planned to return for the equipment he needed after consultation with father. That evening, the three New Canadians settled down beside the mosquito smudge for a long talk.

While the brothers smoked their pipes, mother asked her nostalgic questions about her sisters whom he had recently visited and his own relatives and their mutual friends. The brothers swapped yarns about experiences in Africa and China and news of conditions in Western Canada. Later, while he helped Leo to pitch his tent, father mentioned the journey he must make for his implements and Leo willingly offered to stay with mother, though not until he had inspected his own quarter section.

Unlike the good farming land father had chosen, with less experience and less yearning for a farmer's life, he had acquired a quarter section that was almost entirely a shallow coulee, a remnant of the Ice Age that cut its way eastward toward the Assiniboine River. Miraculously, it was covered with tall, straight timbers that had escaped half a century of destroying prairie fires. Much closer than the Touchwood Hills where father had expected to go for the timbers for our house, the building materials awaited the blazing he offered to undertake while father went to the Fort.

Father welcomed the brief respite from the domesticity of the tent, a side of life at close range for which he had acquired little liking. After he and Leo had unloaded the wagon box and piled and covered the boxes and bales of furnishings and furniture with oilcloth well anchored with field stones, he put the yokes on the oxen and headed south in a holiday mood. Twelve days later he returned with the implements and the mail that had accumulated at the post office since the day they crossed the Narrows two months earlier; among the letters was Leo's announcing the date of his planned arrival. For the first few hours mother was so happy with her letters that she failed to realize all father had brought beside the implements.

Aware that they had barely enough time to prepare for their first Canadian winter, he had bought a large cook stove and a heater for the proposed sitting room and a couple of doors and British Columbia lumber flooring, together with groceries to replenish the supplies that dwindled faster than they could be acquired.

Mother's hope for getting on with the house soared with every minute she spent savoring the new stove and heater and the windows and doors until father, like a surgeon making a clean decisive cut, informed her that the house could not come first as she seemed to expect.

First must come the haying; cutting and drying and stacking tall prairie grass into cocks built to withstand winter's battering. Then the stable; he and Leo were wasting too much time rounding up the oxen each morning, and to build a corral would waste further time. But, he assured her, the house would be under a roof by the time of her birthday, September 21.

Half a century later, I know that if I had been my mother I would have had to fight with myself to resist a growing conviction that the oxen seemed more important than herself and the children. As she did.

Father, of course, had no such doubts about the priority of the stable; the animals would do more and better work with a shelter and a steady supply of suitable fodder. Never having built a sod stable before, or any other sod structure, he enjoyed the challenge so much that he left a description of the event, commencing with the need for a good rain.

"With the aid of the oxen, some fairly heavy furrows of sod were ploughed. These were cut into convenient two foot lengths with a sharp spade, and hauled to the stable site. The corners were packed and the first sods lined from one corner to the next, one layer along the direction of the proposed wall and the next across, bonding the layers as a bricklayer does. A door and window frame were built in as the wall went up, insuring tightness in winter. The completed stable was the practical alternative to buying costly lumber that would have required another long return trip to the Fort.

"If anyone really wants a job where a back-ache is guaranteed, let him try to build a sod stable," he stated emphatically. Each moist sod weighed between thirty and forty pounds and as the structure rose, so did the lift of each. He estimated that they lifted thirty-two loads of sod and two loads of poles to carry the roof.

Mother's contribution to the operation, apart from cooking for the builders and watching the unsightly structure slowly rise, had been her insistence that it be located well behind the projected site of the house.

A W.C., a small garden, a well, haystacks, and a sod stable marked the settlers' progress when at last work on the house could commence, a structure that, by comparison with the Highgate villa, would be little less primitive than the sod stable.

"Brick and lumber were as rare as opera and hot-house grapes," but as they hauled the timbers to the little knoll such luxuries were far from father's mind. Instead, he and Leo cut and hauled the timbers that were long enough and heavy enough to support the walls, the sills, and foundation layers of the main building, each twenty-three feet long with a diameter at least a foot at the butt and nine inches at the top. Even with the advantage of timbers so close to the site, getting them out of the bluff warranted a special note in father's account:

"Both my brother and myself were pretty well hardened by this time, but neither could lift the thick end of such green logs. Being the shorter, I was elected to hold up the butt, after it had been lifted to my shoulder by our combined efforts, my brother to lift and carry the small end."

They did a slow march through the bluff, calling a breather at twenty yards as each rested his end against a tree without dropping the log, a calamity that might crush either of them: "I could feel the veins standing out on my neck and head like cords, but there could be no relief other than the pauses against a tree until we were out of the woods," and then each log had to be hoisted to the wagon gear.

They laid the main sill for the ell-shaped house, ceremoniously pointing it east and west. That main section was to be the sitting room with a bedroom at the east end. The west wing would be the kitchen, facing the view mother could never escape; a pantry large enough to double as a tiny bedroom if the need arose; and another bedroom with a west window. The cellar under the sitting room would be reached by a trapdoor until access could be added from the outside and garden produce warranted it. Already, during rests after lunch they talked optimistically about storing bags of potatoes and other roots from the garden.

Throughout August and the first weeks of September mother had no time for nostalgia or unspoken hopes that the house would in no way resemble the stable. The baby was learning to walk — we children needed constant watching to keep us away from the builders' tools and the possibility of a score of imagined accidents; when she had meals to prepare she tied us to tent pegs with lengths of cotton clothesline.

The arrival of Old Antelope, already considered a valuable friend, eased her worst worry about how to protect the small, precious supply of fresh and salted meat from flies and maggots. The Indian, reared to nomadic life, provided the practical solution of hanging fresh meat on a high pole where the sun cured the surface, a means derived from drying buffalo and other game before it was pounded into the native staple, pemmican. Father's contrived solution, a tall poplar shorn of boughs and fitted with a pulley and line, provided a series of brief pseudo flag-raising ceremonies as long as the fresh meat lasted. Unfortunately, they finished the meat a couple of weeks before they completed the house, and the bacon had to be rationed.

Mother had hoarded the remaining half of a side of bacon hanging in the well beside the butter and milk. Perhaps she had been too anxious about it; the day father and Leo returned for their dinner with the ridge pole that would signal an end to their carpentering efforts, they found her in tears. The bacon had slipped from her hand as she groped for it, lying on her stomach beside the top of the well that held too much water for any of them to attempt a rescue. She sobbed out her story, much to father's relief, because at first he had feared that some accident had happened to her or one of us children.

Prior to leaving England the loss of half a side of bacon would have been no cause for distress. But it had been their most sustaining food for the labor of lifting logs that each day brought her home nearer to completion. As father recalled, "There are some situations comparatively trivial that stand out clearly in the memory, and that is one of them."

Though they had enough food to last until the red-letter day, they often thought of that bacon at the bottom of the well as they sat down at the tiny camp table to canned meat and bannock.

Each log had been notched and raised, fitted one on top of the other without mechanical aid. The openings for doors and windows were framed, and cross poles had been secured to support the ceiling that must await the next trip to the Fort for suitable material. Father hoped these supports would prevent the structure from spreading with the weight of the roof. The symbolic ridge pole was in place and only then did mother realize that the house was to have a sod roof.

The realization almost broke her gallant determination to make the best of their situation.

Father had omitted to inform her about the roof, just as he had earlier omitted to prepare her for the lack of any kind of shelter, assuming that she would know the basic facts of colonial life, including sod roofs. Laying the sod in the rush to complete the house within the promised time, he failed to realize the intensity of her disappointment.

"The roof might have been a lovely, sloping lawn," he conceded, "but the grass had to be laid on the under side. However, it would grow on top next year, and flowers might follow! Almost as soon as the job was completed a good rain fell, and we were proud that none of it came through the roof."

They chinked the countless spaces between the logs with slivers of wood, securing them in places as tightly as they could with a dubious plaster made of clay and water. When not a glimmer of light showed where winter's wind would surely follow, they hung the doors and windows. On the eighteenth of September the builders assured one another and mother that their goal was in sight; they talked about which crates of furniture they should move first, which boxes they would open, "tomorrow, with luck!"

But the prairies typically resented premature plans. On the nineteenth father opened the tent flap to a world of soft white snow that threatened to rob them of all hope of winning their race with the "monster of which we had already heard too much."

The camp table and chairs were blanketed by snow. Snow covered the piles of boxes and bales that held their every possession except the barest essentials crowded into the tent. They were bitterly cold and their bedding was damp. They were hungry, and not all the flooring had yet been laid in the house.

For a long moment father and Leo, roused and amazed at their predicament, looked at one another across the few yards that separated the two tents. But only momentarily. Spurred by the obvious urgency of the situation they rolled back the bedding in our tent, brushed the snow from the table and chairs for which there usually was no space under the canvas and moved them in, set up the camp stove and got water boiling and with it came a little welcome warmth. But they wasted no time over their meal, or admiring the amazingly beautiful world around them. By the time a warming sun had melted most of the whiteness and turned the heavily tramped bare earth around the house into a quagmire, the last floor boards had been cut and fitted into place.

They quit work only when the shortening daylight and a lack of lamps made further efforts impossible. On the twentieth they put up the cook stove in the kitchen and raised the stove pipes. They carried in the heater and set it on its metal fire-protecting base, and joined and secured the stove pipes in the sitting room. They tested both stove and heater to see that the drafts functioned properly, and swept the muddy floors, and only darkness again prevented them from moving indoors. None of them knew whether the early snow meant that winter had arrived or whether the unexpected phenomenon was merely a harbinger of the Indian Summer of which they had read in the immigration brochures.

Next morning the sun shone again. Father formally and gallantly carried mother across the rough threshold of her new home. His only regret was the lack of a length of satin ribbon and a pair of silver scissors with which she could have completed the ceremony.

"The 21st of September arrived, and with great jubilation we moved our belongings from the canvas to a real roof, a roof for the first time since May. Though it was one that looked impossible to anyone from a civilized home, in those days things were of necessity primitive."

On my journey in search of the story of that Wilkins pioneering decade I left the modern highway and followed the trail leading to the front door. Even in a gentle rain, I needed no special imagination to visualize what the ground must have been like two days after the snowfall and despite the warm, drying sun. Sitting in the car to keep myself dry, I made my rough sketch of the layout of the rooms, later checking them from every direction when the rain had stopped. I forgot the passage of more than half a century. In a strange way the front door of the little house became as evocative as Bach's haunting "Air."

If mother had crossed that threshold straight from London she would have loathed the place and everything about it. Instead she celebrated her first birthday in Canada so relieved to be out of the cramped, back-bending tent that she felt an eager longing to "make the best of it" — the phrase that became a sort of creed. She showed father and Leo where she wanted the kitchen shelves and the shelves in the bedrooms. Seated on the kitchen floor on a hastily unrolled and still unread copy of the overseas edition of the London *Times*, she laughed and cried as box after box revealed familiar treasures, holding each up for their appreciation. She unwrapped the silver cruet and the china pastry cup she used for making beefsteak and kidney pies, sauce pans, and the children's silver mugs.

But she could not stay at any chore for more than a few minutes. Every item roused nostalgic memories, and she wanted to see everything at once. With the baby clutched against her hip, she reached down to a half-emptied crate and found the antelope horn they had used at home for a hat rack; it could be hung near the door beside father's sjambok. From the crate clearly marked *first needed* she lifted carefully wrapped china and cutlery, only momentarily sad when she came on several pieces that had not survived months of handling.

When father and Leo had assembled the tables and chairs that had been taken apart for convenient crating, she eagerly watched them unpack and put together the bamboo what-not, the souvenir of the dramatic *The Darling of the Gods* that had started the London rage for oriental furnishings. On it they arranged their most cherished family photos. They argued happily about which pictures to hang, father insisting that there be no unnecessary screw holes in the new logs.

They agreed that the pair of silky African leopard skins that had adorned the little Highgate sitting room had no place in this rough, rude room with the sod roof; they must be stored in the empty pantry until the permanent roof was added. With scarcely a murmur of regret mother rewrapped them in the linen sheet in which they had been sewn. It was the heavy parcel in the same sturdy crate, also sewn into a sheet, that forced her first, and only, nostalgic cry that day, the heavy parcel of her music, the scores of operas she loved and popular songs, the arias and her favorite piano works. With tears blurring the inscription she had so carefully written to identify the contents, she laid it on the lower shelf of the what-not. Like the leopard skins, music belonged to some future time. Now she must not think about it, nor about her piano.

Today it was enough to secure the essentials, and to her a curtain at her bedroom window was an essential; townswoman that she still was at heart, even on the unpeopled prairie she cherished her privacy. Today, on her birthday, she was thankful for a fire in the new stove, light from the new bracket lamp on the wall, supper seated at a real table, and the children's cots reassembled in the tiny east bedroom; and for themselves a real bed that meant an end, she fervently hoped, to sleeping on the ground.

In the urgency of that first excited day they had not realized how much the house would mean to us children, left for as long as possible in the relative security of the still carpeted tent. Before we wakened, during the first morning light, father shook the carpet clean and laid it in the sitting room. Wondering whether I would remember what a floor was like after months of running about on grass, mother watched her eldest daughter scamper across the sitting room, sliding and shrieking with delight, as happily as when she had taken her first steps in the London house. In much the same easy way, Nora learned to walk before anyone remembered to put breakable articles out of her reach.

After preparing our first breakfast, washing our hands and faces in a basin on a real stand as she had washed her own, mother turned to something she had dreamed about daily in the tent, making bread. Four months spent cooking bannock in the frying pan on the camp stove had made her long for a real loaf of crusty, fragrant bread baked in a real oven; it had become a symbol of all she longed for in Canada.

Actually making bread had frightened her. It had been so easy and natural to think about the crusty loaves that came from the baker at home. Faced with the immediate challenge of flour and the various other ingredients indicated on the little package of dry yeast, she had to appeal to father and Leo for advice and encouragement. Together, they proofed the yeast, took turns kneading the squeaky dough, agonized over the exact stages when the dough should be shaped into loaves for the final rising before entrusting them to the new oven, praying that the temperature would be right.

That first batch of bread fell far short of their hopes and expectations, but mother soon baked loaves that filled the house with their fragrance. She had her disappointments when the supply of dry firewood was replaced by green poplar that failed to give an even oven heat, and when a cold spell resulted in dough that remained unleavened and sour. But the disappointments were merely temporary and rare setbacks.

The cold spell was accompanied by prolonged, drifting rain that lasted for several days, soaking through the inadequate plaster until great chunks fell to the floor. Only the miraculous arrival of Old Antelope prevented what surely would otherwise have been sheer disaster; the Indian came to tell them that his people were now burning limestone. Father hitched the oxen to a hastily constructed stoneboat, and when he returned with several leather bags of lime he and Leo painstakingly removed the remnants of mud plaster, replacing it with lime and sand that lasted for years.

When they thought they were ready for winter a glorious Indian Summer reminded them of the unpredictability of the climate in Western Canada. Father recalled it with eloquence:

"During the entire time there was a stillness, almost ominous, and yet amazingly calm and beautiful. Not a single cloud crossed the sky. The days were curiously crisp and yet warm. Clear and cold and brilliant with stars, the nights were jewels of experience to be remembered. It was as though Time's camera had stopped at a particularly beautiful scene. We lived, suspended between an odd sense of peace and foreboding. Not a bird song broke the stillness and when the oxen lowed the sound seemed almost sacrilegious."

Convinced that such weather could not last for long, he and Leo spent hours each day with their guns, enjoying some of the finest sport father had ever known: fat prairie chicken and ducks and an occasional rabbit for a change of diet.

So eager were they all for fresh meat that they cooked a prairie chicken without hanging it and discovered that fresh game was more delectable than game hung long enough to suit an old-country palate. When plucking the birds became tiresome, they skinned them. In typical pioneer dependance on trial and error, they adopted the then unfamiliar-to-them custom of serving a whole bird to each person. With the few vegetables from the garden and a little conserve made from mouth-puckering wild choke cherries they ate "like guests at a Lord Mayor's banquet." When the thermometer dropped to freezing they froze the surplus birds on the north slope of the roof.

That first cold spell denuded the trees of every leaf. The men turned from hunting game to hauling dry wood from the bluffs, stacking the logs in teepees until they could saw them into convenient lengths for the stove and heater. Father spent many an evening cutting and trimming a log with a hockey stick-shaped root into runners for a sleigh, a project that proved its usefulness early in December when the first blizzard struck.

They had thought they were prepared for their first real northwestern Canadian blizzard, but nothing they had known could prepare them for the sudden violent onset of the storm and the fearful force of the wind that threatened to lift the house off its timber foundations and hurl it across the nearest bluff. Father stoked the fires and assured mother that they had wood and water and food enough to keep them snug as long as the storm lasted. Yet even he began to listen to a strange, ominous sound that not even the moan and roar of the wind entirely drowned late on the first afternoon. When the sound persisted, he put on his heavy clothes and went outside to investigate. To his horror he saw flames shooting from the gable above the stove-pipe outlet.

"I rushed back into the house. For several feet the pipe was red hot and crackling. One thinks amazingly fast when the roof overhead is almost on fire, when a terrific blizzard rages, and when there are small children in acute danger."

Help, other than their own, was miles away, but there was a pail of water handy. He seized the brass greenhouse syringe he had brought from England and, nostalgically, hung behind the stove. Using the nozzle instead of the spray, he rushed outside again and quickly doused the flames on the roof. Grabbing a pole from the firewood teepee, he knocked the chimney pipe into the snow. Inside, a large handful of salt checked the fire in the stove.

"The flames from the stove had not been reaching up far enough to cause the blaze, but we soon found what had caused it. The chimney just below the outlet was almost choked with a gummy, black flammable substance (later, I discovered that this resulted from burning green poplar) that smelled like a preparation for artificially smoking pork into bacon." It also smelled like danger.

Next day father set off for Fort Qu'Appelle in the new sleigh, again leaving Leo to look after his family. His main objective was the purchase of an iron jack that would carry the pipe outside and away from flammable woodwork. The hardware man, an old-timer with pioneering experience, advised him strongly against burning green poplar without some dry hardwood and urged him to get in a supply of hardwood from the Touchwood Hills before the real winter set in.

Grateful for the advice, father stowed the new jack in the sleigh and spent another day shopping for staples and for Christmas presents. On the way home, he stopped at the post office for our mail and, as had already become a neighborly practice between them, John Locktie's.

As before, the letters from home moved mother to laughter and tears. She read and re-read them to father and Leo, and they all talked about Christmas days spent together with relatives and friends at home. Their parcels were as welcome as the letters: a plum pudding and a fruit cake; a box of Swiss chocolates; toys and warm garments the grandparents had rightly known would be needed. They were the first of many parcels that were eagerly awaited year after year.

Shortly before Christmas Day a rancher driving north with a load of beef stopped at the house and offered frozen forefronts of beef at five cents a pound and hindquarters at six. Father bought a hindquarter and sawed and chopped it into suitable joints. Saving the choicest rib roast for Christmas dinner, he stored the remainder with the game birds on the north side of the roof, out of the sun and reach of hungry coyotes.

"That first Christmas Day in Canada dawned clear and amazingly mild. We had our dinner at noon-time with the door wide open, and what a dinner it was! Roast beef and the plum pudding our friends at home had so thoughtfully sent us. And a real fruit cake! They had guessed rightly. There was no opportunity for securing such luxuries as the makings for plum pudding and fruit cake. We had a few vegetables grown on the small plot and we scarcely missed the nuts and raisins, the grapes and oranges and sweets which to most people are indispensable at Christmas.

"Solemnly we toasted absent friends and wished many of them might share our adventurous lot." It was the toast they were to make every Christmas as long as mother lived: "To our absent friends!"

Again the fine, mild weather did not continue long. They used to say they survived that first immigrant winter only by thinking of spring and, of course, thanks to the trips father and Leo made to the Touchwood Hills for pine and other hardwood to burn with the poplar.

On each of those trips they left home in the bleak, cold pre-dawn at five o'clock, returning at midnight or later. The oxen were slow. Cutting logs, snaking them out of the woods, and loading them onto the sleigh was exhausting work even for young men in top physical condition. After a hearty breakfast, their only food throughout the long day was frozen sandwiches and tea boiled over a fire in a clearing in the snow. On the home journey, to keep their minds off cold such as they had never imagined, they took turns running beside the oxen and sitting on top of the load, rolled in horse blankets.

Occasionally they met Métis in the hills and from them heard many details of the adventures and hazards of logging. Some of the anecdotes they shared with mother over a cosy, late supper after the oxen had been fed and watered; others they carefully kept from her. They never told her about the two settlers who, during a blizzard, lost their way returning home from a logging trip and were not found until spring melted the snowbank that had drifted over them and their sleigh and animals in the lee of a shallow coulee in which they had taken sanctuary.

For her those logging trips were a nightmare. Her imagination outmatched the grim details she had been spared. Striving to keep us children warm, hour after hour she stoked the fires, anxiously watching the piles diminish in the woodbox as night settled in; terrified that she might not be able to saw and split more if some accident prevented her men's return. All through those dark hours she longed for the merest glimmer of light from another settler's shack, knowing there was none, only the cold, lonely stars that reminded her of the equally lonely song of Tosca's lover from his prison, "The Stars are Shining," a song she could not now think of trying to sing.

The days were never as long as the evenings. She always had washing to do, and she welcomed the opportunity to finish drying garments and diapers, sheets and towels without the usual concern over sparing two men the clutter of hanging them on lines strung across the kitchen and sitting room; with the first hard frost she had given up struggling with frozen sheets out of doors. Most of all during the first winter, she welcomed those relatively few hours that were so comforting to her sense of modesty, the opportunity to wash and dry the neatly hemmed squares of winceyette on which many women depended before the emergence of commercially available sanitary napkins. That feminine chore had been one of her most embarrassing problems ever since the arrival of father's young brother, and even of living in such close quarters with her husband. Above all, she welcomed each monthly reminder that she had escaped a pregnancy she dreaded under their present circumstances.

But nothing, that first winter on the prairies, occupied her time and ingenuity more than trying to keep us children and herself warm.

Often the three adults laughed wryly at reminders that old-country people were blessed with warmer blood than North Americans; that they seldom felt the cold during their first winter in Canada. She spread folded blankets on the floor where we played, hoping to prevent us from catching a chill. She put us to bed in two pairs of the warm English-made Dr. Denton sleepers that had to be dried in front of the open oven. She never used the commode father fitted up behind the chest in their bedroom without silently blessing him. Yet despite her every effort to conserve fuel, day after day he and Leo spent hours at the sawhorse in their heavy outdoor clothes, cutting logs into convenient lengths for the stove and heater. She used to think, as she watched them from the north window, that they looked like three-pronged swastikas with one muffled leg steadying the cross bar, much like the emblem on Rudyard Kipling's books.

Through February and into March brocades of frost ferns made every window so opaque that she had to rub patches clear to see out at all. Pails of water left on the floor overnight froze solid by morning, though they did not freeze if put on the table, a fact that prompted father to bank snow closely about the lower outside walls. The success of that banking of the snow in turn suggested one of their most ingenious experiments.

Well aware that heat rises, father had often looked up at the vaulted sitting-room ceiling that had delighted them during the warmer days of autumn when a ceiling seemed less important than any other improvement. Now he vowed never to pass another winter without enclosing the ceiling space to keep the heat in. They talked about it day after day, like thirsty travellers in a desert recalling cool, refreshing streams, until one of them thought of the linen sheets.

Mother had packed a generous supply of linen sheets, expecting that such a commodity would be scarce in the colony, and not immediately needing them they had stored the still unopened crate in the pantry.

Selecting a couple of the largest, on improvised ladders father and Leo tacked them to the ceiling joists, folding the selvages along the angles with the walls to avoid cutting. Then, desperately hoping that similar means might insulate the walls, mother helped them take down every picture and fold and fit smaller sheets around the windows and doors. As the sitting room gradually became warmer, they marvelled that they had not thought of the solution sooner. They reminded one another gleefully that they had merely adapted the ancient wood carvers' favorite linen-fold design to twentieth-century necessity and decided to do without pictures for a few weeks rather than screw holes through the precious sheets.

The first batch of bread mother set to rise in the comparatively warm room became an added benison to their efforts. Instead of the sour smell of unleavened dough to which they had become inured in recent weeks, they gloated over loaves that rose miraculously and over the crusty bread that filled the entire little house with its fragrance. That day father struck a dramatic pose — he enjoyed striking poses — and sang a lusty "Flowers That Bloom in the Spring, Tra-la." It became a theme song for wakening us all on subsequent cold mornings on the farm.

Mid-March brought longer days, and occasionally the sun melted the ice fronds on the southern kitchen and sitting-room windows. The appearance of the snow began to change, its sharp, sculptured drifts slowly softening to more gentle curves. The dazzling whiteness looked as though it had been sprayed with a mist of gray rain, and mother dressed us in our warm clothes and took us out "for a breath of fresh air." Spring was coming.

The end of winter and the promise of spring meant much more to her than to any of her family. She had not gone farther than a couple of miles from the little knoll since she arrived, nor returned to Fort Qu'Appelle as father had done. For almost a year she had not seen or talked to another woman. During those months, though she had adapted her outlook amazingly well to her new circumstances, she had plumbed the depths of loneliness and longing for feminine companionship.

That late March, if some genie had offered her a single wish it would have been for a neighbor she could occasionally visit, perhaps another English woman; she would have welcomed any one of the newcomers she had seen at the Immigration Hall in Winnipeg, no matter what her ethnic origin.

Year Two

Spring came late, ignoring the promise of those first few warm days, heralded by the tail end of a far-away chinook. Suddenly crocuses bloomed on southern slopes while snow lingered in the bluffs. It was the loveliest, most welcome spring they had ever known.

They had made countless plans for that spring, mother hoping for feminine companionship and for a chance to escape even for a few hours from the confining little house; father to get on the land; Leo for an end to weather that one day reminded him of an English spring and the next brought a return to arctic blizzards.

Father could do something about his longing; he decided to buy another ox. Two oxen could not accomplish the forty acres of ploughing he had set as the season's goal, plus essential fire guards and a new garden plot to replace the original where the soil had proved to be too heavy for most vegetables he hoped to grow.

First he must find the ox, a search that led to several brief excursions and opportunities to meet the few other men in the vast, sparsely settled area. Happily discussing mutual problems and hopes with one of them he heard about his third ox. Acquiring it provided all the diversion he craved.

The owner, a bachelor living in a dreary sod shack several miles away, lacked father's useful African experience with oxen; he had simply given up trying to work with them and hobbled his yoke to fend for themselves until he could find a buyer. He had already sold one, the more manageable beast. Father could have the other if he could catch him, a challenge he accepted as soon as he saw the animal.

With every overture, the ox tossed his proud head and ambled away, furthering the potential owner's determination to possess him. After several attempts, and much as he disliked having to admit to failure, father hired a young Métis to ride out and rope him.

"The splendid beast's captivity began by being hitched by the horns to the back of the wagon, with a strong one-inch rope to prevent him from getting away. As soon as he felt the first pull on his horns he planted his feet firmly, and to our amazement that one-inch sturdy rope stretched until it broke!"

Scotty was roped again and hitched beside the yoke of oxen, father walking on his other side. There was no further trouble until he was introduced to the plough, part of a proposed yoke of "many horse-power oxen, Sandy the heavy one in the furrow, Pat the lighter, on the grass and Scotty between them." Scotty acquiesced for a few yards. Then he lay down and refused to move.

"I was loath to use a whip on him, knowing his nature, but after a reasonable interval, during which we accomplished nothing, I gave him one good cut. He came up like a shot and leapt into the collar, threatening to break harness, plough and everything, and then he stood trembling like a leaf. After that we got along splendidly. He received firm, kind treatment, plenty of good food, and pasturage. Within a few weeks we were managing an acre a day and kept the team up to standard — three oxen, a plough and a man!"

The next acquisition was another cow, purchased from a settler driving his herd farther north along the Touchwood Trail. Because the cow was due to calf, she could go no farther, and for thirty dollars father acquired a Shorthorn crossed with a Jersey. His hopes for a future herd revived, though only briefly. Fanny dropped a bull calf instead of the desired heifer, but her milk was so rich they made more butter than they could use and experimented with cheese. In the autumn the young steer provided a winter's supply of fine, grass-fed beef. With a couple of cows, two pigs, the hens and eggs they already had, and the newly cultivated garden plot, father began to feel that his hopes of achieving his goal might be nearer than he had dared to anticipate.

"We had splendid cabbage, carrots and potatoes. The carrots were available throughout the entire season by thinning, and the thinning left space for later vegetables to mature for winter storage."

They grew exceptionally fine peas too, a natural crop in country where the Everlasting Pea grew wild on the prairie, but nothing equalled the onions in quality and quantity, despite the tears produced by a single package of Yellow Danvers seed purchased at the Fort.

Soon after the seeds were planted, thinning and weeding the seedlings became an endless, backaching chore, partly because father insisted on honoring the Yorkshire principle that a good farmer wasted nothing. In later years there would have been neighbors to whom they could have given bags of onions, and markets; in 1905 when Leo hauled fourteen bags to the Fort, no one would pay more than two cents a pound. The very best of the crop they plaited into colorful festoons and strung them across the front of the house to ripen, so many that mother refused to permit another onion to be brought within smelling distance.

There were several bonuses in that single package of onion seed, seeds unlike any potential onions father had ever seen.

"From them we had the finest beets one could wish, more rhubarb eventually than we could use and several flowers I could easily identify, among them the finest Cinerarias I had ever grown!" Many of the flowers either sowed themselves in subsequent years or were perennials that continued to bloom long after the onion crop had been forgotten.

None of the achievements meant as much to him as the first grain crop he longed for more ardently than he had ever wanted his parchment from his London college. By the end of the second summer he and Leo had ploughed seventeen acres that would be ready for harrowing next spring. Seventeen acres that for father represented more than as many days trudging behind the plough. But they were happy days. As he steadied the single ploughshare and guided the plodding oxen, he thought often of the good advice he had received from the specialists at the Dominion Experimental Farm at Indian Head. They were also long days when the promise of the new, well-established Red Fife wheat seed they had recommended eased his aching back and shoulder muscles as much as mother's patient, nightly massaging. He marvelled that she made the liniment last as long as he needed it, and he told me years later that her firm kneading contributed as much to his first summer's success as a farmer as the actual breaking of the soil. I have often hoped that he told her so.

That summer every plodding step on every new furrow symbolized his intense feeling for the soil and for man's dependance on using it to the best of his knowledge and ability.

"Long before the plough share entered the prairie sod homesteaders had plans for the use of the cultivated area of the future. As they walked up and down those long furrows, slowly suiting their pace to the steady gait of their oxen, they dreamed many dreams and planned many plans. Wheat was uppermost in the minds of most of them as they plodded, their dreams broken only by the occasional half-grunted Gee, Haw, Giddap or Whoa-there! Wheat would bring in cash, real money with which to buy necessities for man and beast; food; fodder; more animal power; more acres, implements and buildings."

But he knew it was oats on which he must depend to keep his hard-working oxen in top condition; oxen needed heavy rations of oats if they were to pull a ploughshare through that tough, virgin grass, the "prairie wool" that produced the famous early bumper crops. With oats selling at sixty cents a bushel at the grain dealers, the next spring he shrewdly sowed part of his fields to this fodder crop, even at the expense of sacrificing income-producing wheat.

"It was during the reverential period of our second summer that the cause of our first community organization occurred."

The first tiny crops were up a good six inches when herds of roaming cattle threatened the clash of interests father had foreseen and feared that star-lit night when he had led mother out of the tent to see the cause of the oxen's restlessness. Bands of horses followed, trampling the last vestiges of the precious, unfenced crops, foraging on wild hay that was equally as valuable to settlers who could not afford to enclose their fields with barbed wire.

It was not an entirely new struggle. As long ago as the arrival of the earliest farmer the clash of interests had been apparent, and though some farmers had appealed to the territorial government for protection, the ranchers claimed their right to the open range that had existed since the coming of the first Indians and the buffalo; if settlers wanted fences they must pay for them. The situation that spelled heartbreak and failure to men who had yet to harvest a first crop naturally brought many of them together. It also brought mother her first feminine companionship.

Regardless of his respect for tradition, the ranchers' attitude outraged father. Unaware that other men in other parts of the Northwest were as incensed as he, he discussed their local situation with every man he met on the trail or more often at the end of a furrow, over a pipe while his oxen rested. The invasion of further bands of roaming cattle led to more talks, until one evening he arrived home for his late supper with momentous news — he had met a new settler's wife, a woman mother would surely like.

Whether the suggestion was his or hers, on the following Sunday — on father's farm Sunday was always a day of rest — he walked the five miles to the newest settler's shack and invited him and his wife to supper the following week. The invitation was eagerly accepted with the suggestion that another newly arrived couple might also welcome the opportunity to discuss mutual problems.

To his amazement when he returned with the acceptance, mother lost her nerve. That entire year in which she had never seen another woman had left her diffident and self-conscious, embarrassed because she had so little to offer. She needed all the gallant reassurance father could muster to restore her poise and her innate love of people. She needed to be reminded that what she had to offer would be exactly what every other settler's wife could produce — a roast of beef, the few early green lettuce leaves from the garden, bread and the butter she churned in a large glass jar with a tightly fitting top, tea, and plain pound cake.

She felt like Robinson Crusoe, completely out of practice in talking to strangers, torn between excited anticipation and the dread that she might actually find herself tongue-tied.

Early that Sunday afternoon a wagon as new as their own had been the previous year rumbled up to the log house with the two couples. Without a moment's hesitation mother rushed out to welcome them, all three women so delighted to meet one another they smothered their lack of coherent words in a welter of tears and laughter. The men escaped the poignant moment while father and Leo showed off their few modest improvements.

In the sitting room, as she presented her children to the English bride and the young Ontarian expecting her first baby, mother felt like an old-timer. She had survived an entire winter and almost two summers on the prairie and they were newcomers. She forgot how much she needed them as she realized how desperately they needed her.

When the children had been fed and put to bed, the four men joined the women around the table covered with a damask linen cloth from home. They talked about their hopes and laughed over the blunders and dismissed the mutual hardships. Before the guests climbed into the wagon for their homeward journey, they had agreed that one of them would take the problem of the roaming cattle to the new government at Regina, whether it was still the old territorial government or whatever succeeded it in the new provincial status of which they had all heard rumors.

For mother as well as her two neighbors — the farthest lived only ten miles away — every hardship had eased with the assurance that she could call on another woman if she needed help or advice, or even to borrow a cup of sugar or a yeast cake.

During the summer of 1905 an incredible thirty thousand settlers swelled the pioneer population of the Territories, though it was later estimated that one-third had left within a decade. Officially, on September the first the territories of Saskatchewan, Assiniboia, and Athabasca became the provinces of Saskatchewan and Alberta in the Canadian Federation.

Like most settlers, our parents gleaned their first impressions of their new political status from weeks-old newspapers from home — in their case the overseas edition of the London *Times* — or from letters that referred to items in European, British, Eastern Canadian, or American papers. Weeks passed before most newcomers subscribed to local Canadian newspapers or received their mail at the nearest post office or mail box and so began to understand local views on the important happening. Fully occupied with the essentials of survival, they relied on sparse, infrequent opportunities for gossip unless, like father, they were thrust into some public aspect of the new life.

He and mother found the word *Saskatchewan* a difficult tongue twister, and grandfather Wilkins always added the letter *r* to it. Despite repeated reminders that it originated from a Cree word meaning swift river, he addressed every letter to *Saskratchewan*; in the quiet Cambridgeshire village to which he had recently retired, it was impossible for him to comprehend either the twelve hundred miles of the river or the spaciousness of the prairies.

While grandfather Wilkins had no great need to understand the problems and challenges of pioneer life on the Canadian prairies, it was different for his daughter-in-law Mary Eleanor. This was her life and she was proud of their new neighbors' suggestion that her husband take the problem of the roaming cattle to the new provincial government at Regina. At the time she could have had no idea that she would come to hate the outcome of his modest entry into local politics as much as she had welcomed it. Probably she never realized, either, how much his three years' experience in southern Africa had prepared him for such a role.

Following his next trip to Fort Qu'Appelle, he announced that he had met W. R. Motherwell, the man who was about to be sworn as the province's first minister of agriculture. The announcement provided mother with a rare glimpse of farm life beyond her own small world; Mr. Motherwell was himself a farmer, living on the land he had settled a decade ago south of the valley. That highly successful farmer — father had taken the opportunity to remind him about the need for a law to protect farmers from the ranchers' marauding cattle — had offered to introduce the local delegate to the new premier, Walter Scott. After watching her husband steer his oxen southward to the Touchwood Trail, whether she sensed his relief in getting away for a few days, mother was overjoyed to welcome him back from the trip to the Fort and his first train journey since their arrival.

She listened avidly to every item of news he shared with her and with Leo, and asked excited questions about Regina. She was as amused as he was when he recounted the amazing information that the premier had received him in a false-fronted, makeshift office, on a plain kitchen chair behind a plain deal table. Even less believable to a woman familiar with pictures of the imposing Houses of Parliament in London was father's description of the Honorable Walter Scott in shirt sleeves; they tried to imagine the premier in Westminster receiving even as modest a delegation as one farmer in less than a frock coat. Mother had not yet become interested in the aboriginal rights being claimed by Indians and Métis, a claim that father upheld, but she warmly applauded the promise of a Herd Law; their own fields would be safe if the ranchers were required by law to herd their cattle between the months of April and October, under penalty of a stiff fine for every infringement.

The excitement of news from the outside world delighted mother almost as much as her joy in having him safely home again.

Splendid celebrations had preceded or otherwise marked the coming of provincial status in towns such as Regina and Battleford, the Qu'Appelles, and as far away as Prince Albert on the North Saskatchewan River, largely because they were close to the railway or other established means of communication. Our little community, now Headlands P.O. from its central location in the township, delayed its celebration because everyone lived so far from everyone else that it took weeks to make the arrangements. Eventually, the proposed visit of a Presbyterian missionary parson suggested a date, a combined first church service and a picnic at the home of the new postmaster.

Much as mother disliked travelling behind the oxen, she packed a picnic basket, dressed us children in our best outgrown summer frocks, and, in honor of the occasion, wore one of her tucked white blouses with a high whale-boned collar and the straw boater that appears in many of father's photos of their outings on the Thames. Because the late September day was almost as hot as July, she wore the coolest of the long dust-ruffled skirts that had been right for many a gay Sunday afternoon in London.

Father paid his enthusiastic tribute to the pioneer event by recording its highlights:

"They came in wagons, some in hayracks, a few on horse back, and one socialite in a buggy. The attire, too, was as varied and under less serious circumstances might have done for a costume affair. A few of the women wore their smart, year-old frocks from the large centers that had been home, others were in shawls. Some of the men wore overalls and one, the owner of the buggy, was a bonnie sight in a frock coat. There were children, one a baby, and two or three 'half-breeds,' " a term father heartily disliked; he soon replaced it with Métis, locally pronounced *M'teese*. As in Africa, and despite his British arrogance, he tended to abhor Canadian racial distinctions based solely on color.

After the brief, informal religious service everyone gathered in the pleasant shade of a nearby bluff for supper, affording father an opportunity to ask each man about his former trade or profession. He found, as well as his brother, a ship's captain, a first mate, and a marine engineer; an architect and a building tradesman; a fabric designer; a captain and a lieutenant from a famous English cavalry corps; "and I straight from Cornhill in the heart of London."

Their ethnic origins were as varied. Among them — and every man in the community was present — he found his Scottish neighbor, John Locktie; the German whose children caused us considerable envy as we grew up because we longed for their lard and syrup instead of the jam we had on our bread; the Jewish couple to whom mother was warmly attracted because they were trying to discover how to move their piano from South Qu'Appelle to their enviable half section; and a delightful family of Hungarian peasants who were soon to be joined by others from their home community.

"Under any other circumstances there would have been a certain stiffness and reserve, but here each man and woman knew what it meant to be lonely." They all introduced themselves. And they all shared the situation that already had become a basic part of father's far-reaching hope for the community:

"There was everything to be done which must be done when men and women get together to establish a social unit; rights and privileges to be established and enforced; roads and other public services to be created and maintained; schools to be financed and erected. There was pioneering to be done at every turn, although the various problems mainly presented themselves gradually and not very dramatically."

Though most of the men were bachelors, just to meet three other women and to renew her acquaintanceship with the original two helped enormously to increase mother's feeling that this was home. The painful loneliness of the first year eased with the realization that other women shared hopes and dreams that seemed so utterly unattainable that she could never really talk about them to father. Yet that realization, coupled with the church service and picnic, drew her closer to father than any material occurrence of their five-year marriage.

Late in the second week in October that increased awareness between them faced a serious jolt, particularly for mother. During the first few hours of a rain storm such as they had already experienced on the prairie, the year-old sod roof remained dry. On the second day the few leaks that stained the linen sheet ceiling were easily contained in sauce pans and a pail. Late that evening the storm increased ominously. Leaks plopped down all over the sitting room until they overflowed every available pot and pan and pail. The pioneers had to move everything possible to the center of the room and, as every yard of protecting oilcloth was stretched to its utmost, turn desperately to their raincoats. Then, as suddenly as it had commenced, the rain stopped. The sun came out. A couple of days with good fires indoors and steady, stiff winds that blew garments and bedding dry on the clothesline relieved the immediate situation, though not the need for a new roof.

But a new, permanent roof would require more than a long journey to the Fort for lumber and shingles. Every ton of sod that had so laboriously been cut and lifted into place must first be removed. The prospect of the inevitable mess in itself was enough to force them to postpone the formidable undertaking until spring, but there was also the stable that must be repaired. Hoping that another such deluge could not possibly occur during the winter months, they eventually agreed to patch the weak spots and decided that father and Leo would get on with the storm damages to the roof of the stable. Father settled mother's hesitant reaction with a reminder of how comfortable they had been last winter with the improvised ceiling; he hoped she could put up with the stained sheets for another few months — but even he failed to see how inadequate the sheets would be.

"We had celebrated our second Canadian Christmas, and had almost forgotten the episode of the flood when something happened compared to which that adventure was a mere bagatelle. One morning when I was going through the mental gymnastics necessary to force myself to get up, dress in a very cold room, light fires and generally start the household into action for the day, suddenly I discovered the house was seriously spreading.

"Why my half-awakened eyes should have strayed to one of the poles originally intended to prevent the weight of the roof from forcing the walls apart, I do not know . . ."

The poles had pulled out beyond the linen fold, threatening to drop the weight of seven tons of sod and every pole up to the ridge on the outer walls. Under such pressure the sheets would not last for seconds. When the walls could no longer support the weight, the entire mass would crush every one and everything. A further spread of a couple of inches meant disaster, and they dared not risk lighting fires that would provide the warmth they all craved because any warmth could melt the blanket of recent snow that had added to the overall weight.

All this father realized in seconds, during which time he also thought of the only immediate solution: mother and we children must go to the nearest neighbor's new house that was even smaller than ours. Mother needed no second warning. While he hitched the oxen to the homemade sleigh, she dressed herself and us and packed a bag of essentials. Leo, who would remain in the house, had already begun to move the furniture to the comparative safety of his bedroom in the west wing.

That late January day, though the thermometer registered twenty below Fahrenheit, the sun shone brightly. On the long, slow, bitterly cold ride its illusion would have invited exclamations of delight had our feet been warmed by several hot stones or bricks. But there had been no opportunity for warming stones, nor for a hot breakfast. With two crying children to try to keep warm in cold blankets and the cold straw cushioning the sleigh, mother had to face the possibility of losing the house and consider the enormous risks faced by father and his brother.

The neighbors, as soon as they heard father's news, hospitably invited us to stay with them as long as we must; it was a visit both women would have enjoyed under less urgent circumstances. Father ate a hurried hot noon meal, said good-bye, and drove back to Leo.

The bedroom in the west wing, which eventually was to be the nursery when Leo built his own shack, was too small to hold every item of furniture and every extra packing case. Besides, it would provide the only scant shelter the two men would have during the entire appallingly hazardous operation. They cleared a patch of snow and put up the tent as an auxilliary storage space. Not daring to risk the warmth it would produce until they had moved the roof, they set up the camp stove in the bedroom, along with a supply of food. Then, they drove the oxen to the Fort for lumber and shingles. It was another of the journeys father used to say he would never forget.

"On the way home we told ourselves that only a tenderfoot would long for a warm house and a hot meal at the journey's end. That was by way of mental preparation for the next week or two in either the crowded bedroom or the tent. Preparing food was the worst problem. Sometimes it took an hour to thaw our bread and other food and melt ice for water to make tea over the camp stove with scarcely enough room to turn around."

They removed the windows to save them from damage, and when they had hacked and chipped and lowered the tons of sod from the roof, nothing remained of the main part of the little house but the walls, stark on the snow-covered prairie. Then began the task of levelling the walls and raising the new lumber ridge pole and the rib-like rafters — another herculean feat father would never forget:

"Using the longer nails wasn't so bad at all, but the tiny shingle nails caused us to warm the very air with our profanity. I had never heard of shingling at ten below. I never want to hear of it again, either, but on that day in 1906 we knew that the ten below might any day become twenty or even thirty below, with the possibility of a blizzard. I recall vividly that handling those pesky nails with mitts on was a problem; trying to drive them in with cold fingers was a whole book of Euclid."

And every day they had to feed and water the oxen and muck out the stable. Though the animals provided enough warmth for themselves, it was not enough to prevent accumulated manure from freezing so hard that it could not be moved until late spring, piling high enough to topple the beasts on to their heads; more than one neighbor they knew had lost a valuable horse or steer under such circumstances.

They completed the roof and a tongue and groove lumber ceiling in only a little more than three weeks — too cold and numb and hungry to realize what they had achieved. Then the doors and windows had to be hung before they could light the fires; the grimy windows could be cleaned when spring brought warmer weather and warm water. With the windows replaced, the eyeless little house again looked like home. All it needed, from the bitterly cold outside, was a lovely blue smoke plume curling above the now well-insulated chimney and the new roof.

Their hands clumsy from cold and mitts, they replaced the stove pipes. Very gently they lit the first kindling wood in the stove; sudden heat could crack the cold metal. When the kindling caught fire around scraps of dry newspaper, they cautiously added small sticks of wood, one at a time until the beneficent warmth rose to cheer them. They watched the damper and felt the stove pipe to make sure the fittings were secure.

As the heat slowly spread through the kitchen and to the sitting room, they moved the heater back to its place on the sheet-metal fire protector, and fitted the pipes and damper. They shredded more precious newspaper, added more kindling, and finally a match from the little silver safety box father always kept filled and usually in his vest pocket. As the second source of warmth spread across the room and into the bedrooms, the two ecstatic men unbuttoned their coats and took off their mitts.

They thawed the last half of the last loaf of bread mother and her neighbor had sent them and the last slices of roast beef, both thoughtfully sliced because the women knew there could be no facilities for slicing anything in those cramped, crowded quarters. Their only disappointment that day — and it nearly broke their spartan control — was the lack of a spoonful of sugar for their hot tea; throughout the ordeal they had been unable to find the sugar, and even now neither could remember where they had stashed it away in their hectic early days without heat.

Then they slept in comfort for the first time in weeks, between blankets on the sitting-room floor, agreeing to take turns throughout the night to check and stoke the fires.

Not even a good night's rest entirely roused their enthusiasm for the chore of clearing away the clods and fragments of sod and hay that had fallen in from the roof, some of the mud already thawing on the floor. They lifted the protecting oilcloths carefully so as to scatter the debris as little as possible, carrying each out to where the wind blew it clean; by the time they had shaken the last cover they had darkened an acre of snow as though a sand storm had swept across it. They moved the furniture back to the places mother had chosen more than a year before and carried in the crates from the tent. Then, while Leo swept the floor and dusted the furniture in an effort to remove the last traces of the disaster, father hitched the oxen to the sleigh and went to fetch his wife and family.

Mother's ordeal, though utterly unlike his, had been almost as grim. For her things might have been easier to bear if the neighbors had been less hospitable, less determined to make her stay seem like the natural, typically prairie situation it was; she might have accepted it almost casually but for her innate distaste for the inevitable lack of privacy. Instead, gratefully and as graciously as she could, she slept across the small living room in the children's bunk; the neighbors' two children and I slept in makeshift beds on the floor. The baby slept beside mother, wrapped in a shawl against the cold outside log wall.

We seven people filled every corner of the tiny house. Mother tried to help with the housework and cooking, endeavoring to suit her English ways to those of the Swedish neighbor who knew none other than those her mother had brought from the Old Country when she and her family settled in North Dakota. She told herself that the baby's diapers really did not need to be boiled, and hoped that the lack of fuller's earth would not cause diaper rash; apparently, it did not. She gladly used Sunlight on her face and hands instead of her familiar Pear's soap. The one aspect of the entire three weeks that she could not make herself accept was the lack of the commode in her own bedroom. The daily necessity of dressing herself in every warm garment she could pile on and going out to the wind-battered, bitterly cold little privy near the stable almost broke her spirit.

The sound of father's sleigh when she heard it crunching across the hard, dry snow sent her rushing to the door, crying out in her delight and relief. She didn't notice his untrimmed beard or the long hair that straggled over his coat collar. She was unaware of her own lank hair and uncurled fringe. Ecstatic with the caress of his rough, chilblained fingers, like each of the other adults, she forgot that none of them had had an opportunity to take a bath since the unheralded arrival of the Wilkins family.

That day the only thing that mattered to all of them, the neighbors as well as our parents, was the end of the ordeal. Father and mother were passionately and silently thankful for survival. When they broke apart, father scooped up us children, one in each arm, and turned to greet his beaming hosts. Then, while he peeled off his heavy coat, he gave them a garbled account of his and Leo's achievements, and the wonderful assurance that again the little house was safe and warm. While he ate his first hot meal in weeks, mother packed our few things, as eager as he to put their long, cold drive behind them.

It was the warmth that welcomed her to her home and the happiest day she had experienced since she first climbed the little knoll. Before she took off our outdoor clothes or her own, she walked up and down the sitting room, her head thrown back to admire the tight ceiling, as beautiful under the circumstances as it was practical. The bedrooms were warmer than they had been with the help of the linen sheets. Leo had unwrapped the leopard skins and spread the larger one on the floor in front of the heater where we children delightedly tumbled over its handsome stuffed head.

Though it was almost supper time mother rehung the sitting-room curtains and the curtains in her bedroom and at its doorway, and Leo's. After supper she searched for fresh sleepers and aired bedding for our cots. By that time the snow water was warm and everyone bathed in the round metal tub, children first and then, while Leo retired to his room, mother herself, followed in turn by the two men. Next day, she promised, she would wash the children's hair and her own, and cut the men's shaggy locks. Tonight she was too tired to do another thing. But what a wonderful day it had been!

In the morning she put a batch of bread to rise beside the kitchen stove. Then father moved the remaining unopened crates from the little pantry, and she watched in eager anticipation. Her joy faded as he opened the first and then another and removed the packing material.

"Many of our most valuable possessions had been lost on the C.P.R. boat the *Bavarian*. . . . No trace was ever found of them. Nor were we able to obtain compensation for the pictures and hunting trophies, rugs and other valuables which apparently just disappeared. Looking about the new house there were many spots where there might have been happy reminders of former days."

But mother had her bundle of music and for her no treasure meant more. Now, she carefully lifted the scores from their linen wrapping and laid them on the shelf father had rigged up above the what-not, well out of reach of their younger, now toddling daughter. Though she had no means of playing any of the favorites, merely to have those sheets and collections eased some of the pangs of nostalgia they evoked.

She had restrained her quick tears as she held the score of the overture to *Les Cloches de Corneville*, and "The Three Little Maids From School" that I now knew as well as she. Seeing the *Kyrie* again as father held it up for her inspection, she broke into sobs, torn between relief that the picture had survived the journey and a sudden spasm of homesickness.

It had been one of their most prized mementoes, that photo he had made on the sunny Sunday outing to Ely Cathedral soon after their marriage. Together they had watched the group of boy choristers emerging from the great stone doorway, chanting the ancient "Kyrie Eleison" that had brought hope and comfort to countless generations of men and women since biblical times. Father had enlarged the photo in his darkroom and mounted it between two sheets of glass bound together by gold-colored *passe-partout*; they had both felt they must bring it with them as a sort of talisman. Eventually, they planned to hang it in the west bedroom window where the late afternoon sun shining through would seem to bring the choristers, and their words "Lord Have Mercy Upon Us," right into the room. The photo of the boys in their white surplices, heads back, hymn books in their hands, remained part of our home as long as mother lived.

That day they rehung the heavy oak-framed engraving of Whistler's *Carlyle*, a picture she never liked because she did not like Carlyle, and the artist's famous *Mother* opposite the antelope hat rack and the sjambok that father used to tell us was his personal symbol of liberty.

He had been on an African safari, on foot as usual, when he came on one of the new fairly well-developed homesteads in the vast area south of the Zambezi and the scene he would never forget. Crouched at the edge of the cotton field a group of Kaffirs watched in terror as a white overseer cut deep welts into the bare flesh of a prostrate naked black boy. He had heard of such inhuman beatings. Seeing it not only sickened father but roused him to fury. Without pausing to think about his words, he commanded the white man to stop, while he grabbed the sjambok from his raised hand. To his own and the overseer's surprise, he offered to buy the whip as a souvenir at a price the man could not refuse. The boy's thanks and those of the other workers rewarded him as he rejoined his own party, their respectful *Bwanas* still warm and rewarding in his ears halfway around the world as he hung the sjambok in our primitive prairie dwelling.

During the next few days he put up shelves for many of the other treasures that had survived. Mother's gold and blue china, of which only half a dozen pieces were unbroken, they put on the top shelf, a reminder of the days when the entire tea service had adorned the dining-room sideboard father had made for the Highgate villa. The African diary addressed to *My Dearest Nellie* became part of the shelf of books that we all actually treasured more than the missing carpets we children never remembered having seen. In the remaining space above the shelves they hung the framed certificate of father's admission as a Freeman of the City of London. That certificate provided its very special moments when they reminded one another that no matter what might happen to their prospects as settlers — father never actually admitted to anything but a bright future — their sons would be educated by the hoary old guild to which he belonged. His signature below the seals of the guild and the City of London reminded him of the proud day when he had written it in the Doomsday book of records in the ancient Guild Hall presided over by the effigies of Gog and Magog.

In a cosy home with a delightfully warm bedroom — not since her return had she seen her breath indoors except first thing in the morning — mother felt she could at last confide the secret she had hoarded since the threatened disaster; she was again pregnant.

For the first time since she had known, she could talk about it. Before Christmas she had tried to tell herself that her queasiness and unnatural fatigue had been the result of the dreary clean-up following the three-day deluge. She remembered the night when she had conceived and with a secret female smile the utterly sensual mundane pleasure with which she had enjoyed him after a promise of a real roof in the spring. When Christmas came, she had tried not to think about it, hoping she had made a mistake. During the weeks following the threatened collapse of the hated sod roof, only the comforting companionship of her neighbor had saved her from sheer panic.

She wanted a son. She had sensed father's unspoken disappointment at the arrival of each of their two little girls; she knew how intensely he longed for an heir who would inherit the homestead he was determined to establish. She would actually have enjoyed her pregnancy but for her increasing fear of what could happen to her children if she miscarried on one of the few occasions when she had to be left alone.

She tried to remind herself that a settler's wife must expect to stay alone with her children, that only five months remained until July when the baby was due. She tried desperately to hide her moments of fear when the men left home on each of their early-morning logging trips, not to seem too relieved when they returned late at night. She knew how badly she had failed when father told her that in future they would go separately, taking turns because they had made arrangements with a

Métis to cut and snake out the logs from the bluffs in the hills. She felt more grateful than she could express for their gallantry.

Even that thoughtfulness on their part could not match her relief when father came back from visiting a remote settler with the announcement that he had been offered — and had bought — "a fine team of horses, for $225.00, geldings, mostly Percheron; Prince the heavier horse, was seven years old; King, the lighter, only four."

When the team arrived the following day she and Leo shared father's satisfaction in this latest acquisition. Now he would use the oxen for heavy work such as ploughing virgin sod, a plan he was later to revise; with the horses he could take her to visit the women she longed to know, and when her time came they could get help within a couple of hours.

Though he actually never talked about her fear of being left alone, they both knew that what she feared most of all was that some accident should befall him; with the horses his logging trips would at least take less time. Fortunately, she had no knowledge of the hazards that threatened a logger not yet familiar with handling a team under winter logging conditions until father nearly lost his life.

"The first time I took them to the hills we made the trip in record time, got the load out easily, and made the exhilarating run down to the level of the lake.

"Pleased at the successful day, I led the horses to a hole in the ice for a drink. Prince drank without difficulty, but King did not enjoy having to reach down below his level, although he must have been thirsty. And it was here that I learned the truth of the ancient saying, 'You may lead a horse to water, but you can't make him drink'.

"By persevering I had managed to get his head down to the water level, still hoping he would drink. I was coaxing him when suddenly, with a wild whoop and a yell to his team, another wood-cutter dashed down the slope and across the ice. King jumped, startled, flung back his head, and I was in water up to the knees."

Without realizing the trouble he had caused, the other logger used the momentum of his downhill dash to climb the other shore; with his whoop still ringing in father's ears he disappeared into the star-lit night. The echoes had silenced by the time father managed to heave himself on to the ice surrounding the hole, clinging desperately to the bridle he had gripped as he tried to coax King to drink.

In minutes he could feel his trousers and heavy socks stiffen against his legs. The fire he quickly made on the shore only partially eased his numbness and he knew it would take hours to complete the drying. Cheered and only slightly encouraged by the warmth, he decided to make for home as quickly as he could, running beside the team to prevent the frozen garments from immobilizing him like some ancient suit of armor.

"Fortunately, the tune which I always remembered when my teeth were chattering on the prairies came back to me. Alternately I whistled and sang, 'The flowers that bloom in the spring, tra-la.' Gilbert and Sullivan surely never dreamed that their immortal songs would be sung to a team of homeward bound horses, after dark, with the thermometer somewhere about thirty below, and by a half-crazed man. Music may calm the savage breast, and it does cheer the weary and those in a plight."

John Locktie, knowing that his neighbor had taken the horses to the hills for the first time was waiting and with Leo came out as soon as father whipped his team into the yard. Immediately, the two realized what had happened. While Locktie took charge of the horses, Leo helped father into the house, amid mother's horrified cries that eased when he told her to empty half a can of coal oil into the tub. That night only Leo's excellent naval training in first aid under arctic as well as tropical conditions prevented father from rushing to the heater's warmth. Knowing that a sudden change of temperature could cause disastrous crippling to seriously chilled limbs, with mother's help he forcibly held him back in the cool air beside the door until Locktie came in. Then, as the frozen garments slightly softened and the gradual warmth reached father's feet and ankles, they cut away the socks and moccasins and sponged his feet and legs with the coal oil.

"Thank God, my feet began to tingle. Gradually, feeling returned." He tried to stand up, tentatively at first and then with blessed realization that he could put his weight on them, he knew he still had the full use of his legs.

"One has to face situations of this sort to appreciate the whole hearted relief of knowing that you are intact, and not a maimed encumbrance where a bread winner is needed for your wife and family!"

Mother, four months pregnant, echoed his thankfulness, grateful that it was his last trip of the season. But the experience had helped her to realize how much she must steel herself to meet the shocking challenges of their new life. When Leo left for the hills a few days later, she gave him his hearty breakfast, cut huge sandwiches, and with father repeated the warning about standing close to a water hole while trying to persuade a horse to drink through the ice. She could never understand his or father's enthusiasm for logging, nor their disdain for its risks. She would never have understood her husband's later tribute to that aspect of homesteading.

"Given two or three homesteaders together with their horses and sleigh bells on a bright day, logging was a fine adventure. The highlight was always the swift exhilarating dash down to the frozen lake and across it. Even the horses seemed to enjoy that bit of sport."

As father and mother looked foward to their third spring and summer and their first paying crop, their only concern was mother's pregnancy, and that seemed less worrisome than it had in February, at least to father. Though she had not seen the doctor at Fort Qu'Appelle, father had described her condition to him and had been assured that everything seemed normal.

Year Three

My parents were family people. A home and particularly a farm home without children was unthinkable. To my London-born mother, in 1906 the idea of birth control was abhorrent; demimondes and either the very poor or aristocrats who belonged to another world might use their homemade sponges or whatever it was that they obtained from under the chemist's counter, but not decent middle-class women. Abortion was equally out of the question. Besides, father believed in the ancient biblical insistence on a man's duty to be fruitful and populate the earth. The threat of a population explosion was still decades away.

My parents were also blessed with normal, healthy sexual appetites; not only did father know his wife in that ages old sense, but, as some women have done since men and women began to comprehend their dependance on one another, she knew her husband. How else could they have created the environment that was so immensely happier than its limited resources would suggest? How else account for the fact that she remained an emotionally stable woman despite her frail constitution and the farm's lack of nearly every amenity? Of practically all social contacts?

Anyone who lived on the prairies during those early pioneering years could name women who came west full of hope and enthusiasm and years later died in primitive nursing institutions. The agonizing loneliness, day after day without seeing another woman, night after night without a glimmer of light from another homestead, exacted its toll.

Father talked about some of them, many years later when time had eased the pain of remembrance. Trying to make his voice sound quiet and reasonable, he described the experience of one particularly unfortunate woman who "came out to her man and found conditions hitherto unimaginable.

"They say solitude either makes or breaks a man, but I doubt if the man I am thinking about was much of a man to break. He must have had some means, for his harness and horses and vehicles were of the best, and well kept. Not so his shack or his own unkempt person.

"That man met his English bride's train in overalls, unshaven and with a wagon instead of the decent democrat he might have used. Shocked by his appearance, her first thought was to return to England immediately. But there was no train until the next day. She knew of no place to stay in the strange cluster of shacks near the railway station. She was also the youngest daughter of a cultured but very poor clergyman. In desperation, she turned to the only familiar face she had seen since leaving home, hoping the man was as gallant as he had seemed when she agreed to marry him. She knew better when he took her to the clergyman for their wedding, still in his filthy overalls and, presumably, later to an equally filthy bed.

"When we first met her she was a lovely pink and white and golden woman, welcomed by my wife immediately. Within a couple of years she was faded and worn and unequal to returning home as her friends suggested. She would have been entirely alone two days after her first confinement and in zero weather had it not been for the visit of neighbors, knowing her situation.

"Under happier circumstances this woman, talented as she was and charming, could have been so happy and added so much to the brighter side of our little community. Her romance ended in a mental institution, still on the prairies with the wind she couldn't bear."

Fortunately such situations were rare. There was none of that callous disregard in our home, despite our parents' so different personalities. Through all the family legends and recollections there is no echo of the cynical charge that pioneer couples "had nothing else to do during long winter nights." Though her children, lacking experience, took for granted mother's occasional happy morning smile and father's seemingly unjustified air of owning the whole world, they sensed that their parents shared something wonderful, something they could look forward to as a lovely, enviable right when they grew to womanhood.

For mother, having a baby in a log house on the prairie was very different from having one in London. She had dreaded the prospect of travelling with two children on that long journey by ship and the new railway that father talked so much about. Before Nora was born, naively she had felt they might be taking enormous risks in taking me to that remote colony. Yet she was torn between loving him and voicing the fears that she had begun to realize would anger him if she persisted. Hoping he would come to appreciate the difference between their present comfortable life and the discomforts and hardships of emigration, she had listened to his accounts of meetings in the City with journalists who had been to Canada and with Lord Strathcona and Mr. Sifton. Evening after evening she watched him read about those millions of acres of free land in the newspapers he brought home. Invariably every paper she picked up in the sitting room was folded back to some reference to Canada until in the early months of her second pregnancy the sight of them became a nightmare. Lacking anyone who could tell her about pioneer conditions, her imagination magnified every aspect of rearing two children in so uncivilized a land, and among savage Indians. She became obsessed with the belief that the casual nomadic life that had suited father as a bachelor was not for a married man with a family.

When the London midwife arrived and mother moved into the carefully prepared spare bedroom for her second confinement, she expected a difficult birth and, as every other woman would have done at the time, blamed it on her anxiety. As the hours dragged on, father took the midwife's advice and stretched out on his bed with me beside him for comfort to us both, determined to stay awake until he heard the welcome cries of his son and heir. But the vigil was long and he fell asleep, rolling over on my cherished rag doll and squashing its waxen face beyond recognition. My wails, when I wakened, according to mother's descriptions, were louder than those of my new sister who, because of her cloud of dark hair and out of gratitude to the pretty Irish midwife, was named Frances Nora. Any disappointment father may have felt was mollified by his hope for better luck next time.

The incident of the doll was characteristic, though no man could have wanted or tried more whole-heartedly to care for his family, or to provide for them. He had made the brass-bound rosewood box to hold our infant clothes, his craftsmanship as skilled as that of a professional cabinet maker. He had also made the bassinet mother trimmed with *point d'ésprit* and pink satin bows. He had spent hours taking photos of the first chubby child and longer hours developing the plates, as he did of the second. Yet he could not understand his wife's apprehension at the prospect of bringing up her family under primitive conditions that even the most persuasive Canadian government brochures did not trouble to disguise. A typical Edwardian English husband, he attributed her fears to a natural feminine mood that would pass when she recovered from her lying-in.

Now, settled in the Northwest and facing her third confinement, all those earlier fears again assailed the lonely woman. The wind troubled her, day after day so strong she could scarcely stand against it; clean and astringent and making her long for a whiff of acrid London fog with all the dear family comfort it invoked. Sometimes it seemed beautiful as it bent the poplars with their restless leaves, patterning the grass with movements that reminded her of a Russian ballet dancer and of a Russian ballet itself — cruel, hateful, and at the same time clean and empty as it whipped her skirt about her heavy body.

Indoors, out of the wind, she forgot it as she watched father's thinly veiled efforts to maintain a confidence he clearly did not feel. During the final weeks of waiting they actually vied with one another in their determination to disguise their mounting anxiety.

The hay was made and stacked, work that was his great consolation.

The last rows of green peas were planted in the garden and the harvest imminent though not due to commence for a good couple of weeks when they knew her time had come. She could not have chosen a more convenient date than the twenty-first of July.

"The expected arrival of our first young Canadian caused many hours of grave concern," he told their third child many years later. "Such an event had been viewed with the customary alarm in England, with every facility and the best obstetrical advice of the time.

"Of course there was worry and consternation when a new settler was about to make his debut. But, miraculously it would seem, in the light of the expert care deemed indispensable to the average later twentieth-century city-dwelling woman, many births took place without a doctor and with no thought of a hospital, and often without a trained midwife in attendance. Probably the virility of the men and women who sought the life of a pioneer was largely responsible."

While Leo drove the horses to summon the doctor from Fort Qu'Appelle, and father literally ran for the midwife neighbor, mother stayed alone with us children and the too-vivid rumors that raced throughout so sparsely settled a neighborhood. She could not forget the woman who had had her baby without even the birth chair to which she had been accustomed in her native Middle European village, catching the child in her own hands and cutting the cord. Such terrifying experiences became the nightmares endured by many a pioneer woman who lived through her ordeal, as commonplace as the many accidents.

Mother herself had fallen down the dark cellar steps only a few weeks before, and there was no way she could know what complications that fall might have on herself or her baby; what would happen to her two small daughters if she suffered some permanent disability; if she did not survive her ordeal, a too likely possibility in 1906.

She had not considered going to the nearest hospital at Regina, twenty-four hours away. Like most prairie women, she preferred the familiarity of her own primitive home to the unknown hazards of a journey over rutted trails and the risk of missing the train at South Qu'Appelle if they were delayed by bad weather or a broken axle. Instead, there was Mrs. McPherson, the wife of a newly arrived settler neighbor, said to be a graduate of a famous Edinburgh midwifery hospital. Mother liked and trusted the gaunt, middle-aged, six-foot Mrs. McPherson the minute father ushered her into the house. Her hands, she soon realized, were kind and firm. Her heart was great, and she knew what to do. Without fuss and with very little comment she took charge of the household.

Of course father liked her, even though not an hour passed when he did not look down the trail for the doctor's democrat, all the while knowing that the man from the Fort could not arrive until late the next day. He was grateful for the necessity to keep boiled water ready on the stove, as Mrs. McPherson directed, and for mother's earlier, repeated orders to look after the fractious children who sensed that something strange and desperate was happening.

We were asleep where he had put us on Leo's temporarily unoccupied bed when he heard the piercing scream that could mean only one thing and in a cold sweat he waited for the other sound, the cry of a new life announcing its birth. It seemed hours since Mrs. McPherson had tersely demanded the boiled water before she again lifted the bedroom curtain. Her intent look as she pushed by with the tiny bundle in her arms frightened him.

But the plucky woman who had allowed only that one sharp cry to pass her lips lifted her wan face for his kiss, her gray-blue eyes that always looked too large for her face now larger than ever. Under the white counterpane, her slender, fine-boned body might have been that of a child as she lay back on her pillow. She was all right, she assured him in a whisper he had to lean close to hear; it was the baby she was worried about.

Mrs. McPherson was obviously worried too, but she was competent and calm. She had seen babies as blue as this one, babies who had survived, and she called to father for help. Somehow they must find a suitable warm place for several hours. Did he think he could keep the oven at an even low temperature? Father assured her that he could, and when she had tested it with her bare, bony elbow, gently she laid the little bundle in the soft woollen blanket on the lowered rack — an improvised incubator. Only then did she and father return to the bedroom.

They had to bend close to hear mother's whispered query. But only after she had been assured about her baby did she ask the question that is as old as begetting and bearing children: was it a boy? Or a girl?

Mrs. McPherson's innate good sense and competent training saved both parents whatever hesitation they might have detected in her answer; the baby was a bonnie girl who would soon be as rosy and healthy as her sisters. Father had no opportunity to voice any disappointment he may have felt as he gripped mother's hand, nor to glimpse the desperately relieved woman's fleeting look ahead to the next time.

When the doctor arrived, hours later, he assured them that mother and her baby were doing well and he congratulated Mrs. McPherson warmly. Her ingenuity had probably saved the life of Sylvia Louisa, already named after father's only sister.

They faced an emergency of an entirely different nature before mother was allowed to get out of bed. Mrs. McPherson, competent though she was, had one human frailty: she depended on snuff. She had sniffed her last dram of the stimulant and without snuff she was distraught. The comfortable atmosphere of the little house began to change; mother became restless and the baby who had progressed so well, developed colic. Desperately, father realized that a return to peace and quiet depended on him.

"She asked me to send to town for a replacement. But town was a sixty-mile return journey and our harvest season was almost due. Poor woman, she actually suffered as the stuff had to be rationed out to every other rest period. When it was all gone her quiet competence seemed to go with it."

Faced with this desperate situation father hoped he could provide an acceptable solution, perhaps in a three-pound roll of the famous Hudson's Bay *Perique* tobacco.

"If I could only powder the hard roll it might make snuff. As if in answer to the poor soul's agony I cut the tobacco in half with a fine tooth saw for easier handling, leaving a tiny scattering of dust. It might do. Carefully, I gathered it up and presented it to our precious, gaunt old nurse.

"One long eager sniff! I had to step back or she would have fallen on my neck. Apparently it was heavenly dust. She never tired of praising the stuff, and, as our household returned to order, I too praised it."

We were to hear the story of the snuff often in later years. It invariably recurred, sometimes imaginatively embellished, as he talked about Sylvia's birth. Yet there was no mention of a photo of her or of mother, and I have often wondered why. He had his favorite camera with him. If he had lost his developing equipment along with the other settler's effects, he had had ample time to order and to receive replacements from London, as he had regularly done through the African port of Durban. In that third year, his farm seems to have supplied the satisfaction he formerly had derived from his artistic profession.

Mother certainly had no time to remind him of photographs. No time to remember the convalescence and cosseting that had followed the births of her earlier children. At the end of two weeks Mrs. McPherson returned to her husband and the house they must build before winter. From that day on mother prepared meals for five people as well as nursing the baby, with little assistance from father who was away day after day with his harvest or on some of the new municipal affairs that were beginning to absorb much of his time.

Though she dressed the baby in a minimum of garments that would have shocked her sensibilities at home — on warm days it was no more than a diaper and a binder and flannelette barracoat — she spent hours bent over the washtub and the corrugated scrubbing board. She had barely washed and dressed Nora and me and swept the floors when she had to get dinner ready, with no time for weeding the garden or playing with us as she used to do. Fortunately, her strength returned, one great blessing of the fresh air and exercise that had eased her confinement, and with renewed strength a return of her usual high spirits. Despite the overcrowding of the house caused by the new bassinet father had made,

Sylvia very soon became a happy baby, loved and to her older sisters a wonderful new source of delight.

They dated their prairie life from that late spring day of their arrival, and the high point in Year Three was Sylvia's birth, which only briefly interrupted the farm's steadily developing routine. Father had twenty-eight acres under cultivation, and his first wheat crop ripened without mishap, easily fulfilling every promise in the immigration brochures. With the oats still in stook, and while uncle Leo hung the windows in the new frame barn they had built months before to shelter the horses, in September he joyfully bagged the golden grain and with his first paying crop set off for the elevator at the Fort.

He was on his way home, less than ten miles from the farm, when he smelt the first whiff of burning prairie grass. The sweet, acrid smell forced him to flog his horses; he said later, "If there is a more heart-breaking form of suspense than waiting for a prairie fire to attack one's little family and possessions I have not met it!"

The prairie fire season usually occurred in the few weeks before snowfall when the grass and stubble were as dry as tinder. Everywhere the stage was set for devastation of the whole year's crop. The merest spark could start a conflagration.

Even if Leo could manage to protect the family and the farmyard, nothing he could do would save the remaining field of grain still in the stook. Driving desperately against time, father thought of every dire possibility as he remembered his only experience of fighting a prairie fire, the occasion a year ago when he and every available man within miles had tried to save a new settler's shack and stable.

At first the smell of grass smoke had seemed almost pleasant, an impression that swiftly changed when darkness fell and the glaring, threatening flames became a page out of Dante's *Inferno*. The flames that earlier had raced through the grass now seemed to reach to the stars. The men had checked the newly ploughed fire guards, making certain that not a blade of grass remained that would provide a stepping stone for the flames, and then they had taken up the only weapons they had — moistened grain sacks.

In their potentially mixed farming area, dotted with clumps of poplar and willow, they had learned to adapt their fire-fighting equipment to its conditions. They could not, like ranchers on the open grass range, rely on the efforts of a cowboy riding close behind the newly burnt area, blotting out the flames with the carcass of a steer killed for the purpose. In our semi-parkland at the edge of the Palliser Triangle, wet grain sacks flailed by men on foot became a similar, though an immeasurably more dangerous, device.

Driving his team, father could again feel the heat of those flames and the ache in his shoulders as he flailed at the demon with his wet sack; the agony of his feet when the hot grass charred the leather soles of his boots; the excruciating pain in his eyes and his seared brows.

Now, grateful for the fact that his horses were relatively fresh and his home-going load light, he lashed them unmercifully through wedge after wedge of flames. Sometimes he was surrounded by fire. The sound of sharp, crackling flames devouring dry shrubs and poplars heightened the nightmare. The smoke burnt his nostrils and the smell of the horses' singed manes sickened him. Animals raced by — foxes and badgers and even a deer. Only the birds seemed to escape.

"Seven times the horses were driven through that hell before we crossed the last line of danger and I saw the farm still intact. Thank God, the fire had passed us by that time. . . ."

Between the two rows of ploughed fire guards around the yard mother stood poised with matches in her right hand, ready to back-fire as soon as uncle Leo gave his order. Her skirt was hitched up about her waist, a scarf knotted about her hair, a dripping grain sack clutched in her other hand. Leo had already gathered up every grain sack father had not filled with wheat and saturated them in tubs of water pumped from the well. Together they had carried every moveable article from close to the house, everything that could catch fire if a wind-blown spark touched it. They had both been so intent on their preparations, so blinded by smoke and desperation, they had not realized that the fire had passed them by to the north, though already the sky in front of them to the west had begun to lighten.

Uncle Leo waved a jubilant, sopping grain sack about his head as father's sweat-lathered team thundered into the yard. Mother fell into father's arms as he jumped down from the wagon, sobbing her relief, still so tense that for minutes she could not relax the hand that clutched the matches.

Their escape had been miraculous. Father's arrival was the only help that could have saved them from a last refuge in the slough if a beneficent wind had not changed the course of the fire. It would take hours, they each knew, to piece together all that had happened, hours before the smoke entirely cleared and the sky again assumed its familiar muted autumn blue.

After the first agonizing moments mother rushed into the house to us two terrified little girls and the baby screaming with hunger. While uncle Leo watered and rubbed down and fed the horses and father quietened Nora and me with bread and butter and jam and milk, mother sat down in the rocking chair and opened her blouse to the nudging, searching infant mouth.

But no milk came. None of the milk that normally by now would have saturated the blouse and her chemise and corset. There was nothing for the baby, and no relief from her own numbing agony that was worse than the worst toothache she had ever known. Her breasts felt hard and tight, the nipples excruciatingly painful. The smell of smoke in her hair and on her clothes sickened her, and the crackling sounds of flames that had been less than a mile away echoed in her ears. Remembering the possibility of having to wade into the slimy slough with the baby in her arms, she felt a terrible shudder take hold of her entire body, and the terror of it made her long to scream, knowing that somehow she must relax her awful tension.

She did not scream. It was the baby who screamed again, frustrated and hungry. Across the room father sat at the table with us two older children. She herself sat in the now familiar rocking chair and as she moved with it from sheer habit she began to croon, not conscious of the melody or the well-known words that were part of her being. Slowly, as the melody took charge of her mind, she massaged her taut breasts and though for minutes she did not realize that the miracle had occurred, she felt the guzzling little mouth draw the first welcome drops. The flood of milk brought unspeakable relief. The gossamer touch of the baby's caressing hands assured a complete return of the natural function. Some day, mother knew then, she would sing again.

They were all in bed before dark, mother exhausted and enjoying the cry she so desperately needed to relieve her tortured nerves, the need that father sometimes uncharacteristically seemed to understand.

Like the lovely mornings that so often ease the worst and dreariest of prairie hardships, dawn brought a crisp autumn day. The wind had blown away the sickening taint of burning grass and brush. While mother watched from the back door, father and uncle Leo crossed our ploughed field to see the extent of the blackened swaths where the fire had passed us by. When they returned, grim-faced, their boots blackened with soot, she had to press them to describe what they had seen.

Neither could talk about the extent of the desolation and its significance. Instead, father said that the grass would grow green again; that a prairie fire actually helped to prepare the virgin land for the plough, enriching it with a beneficent layer of charcoal; with rain and a warm October, the grass might show green again before the first snow fell. It was the sight of the dead wild animals they could not talk about, the tiny charred mounds that had been a badger or a coyote, the larger gruesome remains of an antelope.

She had walked to meet them, Nora and I clinging to her hands. Torn between thankful relief for their escape and revulsion at the thought of the sights the men so obviously could not describe, she turned to look at the little house and the W.C., the stable and the barn, and something happened to her. The scene that bore no resemblance to the fine thatched roofs father had talked about or the comfortable Yorkshire house of his dreams, was now her home and the birthplace of her first Canadian child. Nothing could make her admire or love the house she had struggled valiantly to save, but it was all they had, their entire material possession. It was home and the alchemy of danger had opened her eyes to something she had never wanted to understand or appreciate.

She had never shared her husband's dream of a new-world farm patterned on the old; that was his dream and she hoped it would be his achievement. But while it was happening, while he ploughed fields and harvested crops and talked about roads and a school and community development she began to feel that she too, in her own way, could make a contribution that would enrich their lives. It might only be through that pile of scores of her favorite music, for already, and especially on this crisp, stimulating morning after their ordeal, she had begun to sense that this potentially rich, raw land needed more than hard labor. Without songs those millions of acres of free land had no real future, no tomorrow that mattered to her own or the children of other pioneer women.

After dinner father and his brother went to see how Leo's quarter section of poplar had escaped; they could see that the fire had passed John Locktie's bluff and the farmyard beyond it. They were home again well before supper time, quiet and subdued. The flames that had missed our place and Locktie's had swung to the southeast, forced by the wind toward the coulee. Not a tree remained, though some were still burning. As they sat down to their meal the younger brother spoke the words father had expected, and feared:

"This is the life for you, old man. It's not for me!"

Leo wanted more than drudgery, more than this country promised him, much as he had enjoyed their years together. If he was ever to build a house of his own and establish a farm, he wanted a kinder climate than that of Western Canada. Oregon, perhaps, or British Columbia by the Pacific Ocean. Even if he had fulfilled the terms of the land act — and that he had not done — his was not land that father would ever wish to acquire.

For us children uncle Leo became no more than a memory. In time the photo of the tall young man in his naval uniform was replaced on the what-not by a newer likeness of some other relative.

Mother saw him go with mixed feelings. He had provided welcome company during father's various absences, and he had shared her ordeal of the fire. He had often helped her out of trying situations; she thought of the shocking moment in the spring when she had gone to the new stable to gather eggs and in the semi-dusk had put her hand on a snake in one of the feed boxes. Though father had teased her about it, telling her and us children that a harmless garter snake had as much right to like pullets' eggs as we, Leo had taken over the chore ever since. He had helped on the trips to the hills and with cutting timbers and building the house. But while she would miss him, she welcomed the bedroom for Nora and me.

When they had moved in from the tent, the house had seemed

comparatively large. Now she had wondered where she could put Sylvia's bassinet during the cold weather when everyone must spend so much time indoors. She needed some place where we could play, somewhere to put our clothes, somewhere where we could be put to bed at night without crowding her and father's room.

She hung the engraving of the beautiful Queen Alexandra and her grandchildren and the handsome white borzoi dogs on our wall; it was the first thing I saw every morning above Nora's dark head. The smaller leopard skin became our bedside rug, covering the narrow space between our bunks, warm on cold mornings. The *Kyrie* hung at the west window, and late each afternoon as the sun shone through it we learned the words and the lovely old tune. Father's bedtime stories and mother's songs, together with the pictures and the leopard skin, gradually came to suggest a sort of storybook world far beyond anything we could otherwise have imagined. With our own bedroom, a place to hang our clothes, and a place to play, Nora and I began to feel like little girls and no longer like babies.

I felt like a particularly big girl the day mother let me hold Sylvia. She told me to sit well back on her rocking chair. My short, fat legs stuck out in front. She laid the baby in my arms, and I in my excitement lurched forward, rocking the chair and dropping the precious bundle on the floor. Fortunately the chair was low, and the leopard skin near it. When mother let me try again, carefully telling me not to move, I learned my earliest lesson in forgiveness and understanding and I never dropped the baby again.

Christmas that year was particularly happy. We had the usual presents from England and others brought by father from the Fort. Nora and I hung up our stockings beside our beds, with a tiny white sock for Sylvia, now affectionately known as Sybbie. Sylvia's sock was too tiny for the most amazing present we older children had ever held in our hands. Father had bought some oranges. We had never seen oranges that we could remember. We thought they were balls. We ate them only after he peeled one and he and mother playfully smacked their lips, but the little family scene upset mother. She sounded very serious when she told father that we were growing up like ignorant little heathens, and that it was time they thought about our schooling.

What followed her comment remains with me as the first time I really remember how adroitly father invariably changed a subject he was either not ready for or did not wish to pursue. The oranges, he said, reminded him that the dealer at the Fort planned to bring in from the east a couple of gramophones — if he could be sure of buyers. The dealer had told him about the possible purchase as he bought the oranges, and father had immediately ordered one of the instruments.

Of course mother forgot about schools for the exciting moment. Like father, she had a fine sense of timing and she also sensed that there could be few more significant material expressions of his love for her than that he should realize how poignantly she had been starved for music ever since leaving London. She also knew that it would give him much pleasure, if or when the gramophone actually arrived.

"If. . ." How often she had heard that word since coming to Canada.

She had listened to a gramophone, aeons ago in London, dismissing the invention as a travesty of real music on a stage or in someone's home. At the time father had prophesied that they would hear improvements so vast that she would not distinguish between the original and a recording. Then, it had not mattered how much the gramophone improved. Why should she want to listen to *La Bohème* or *Tannhäuser* coming from a huge horn, when father could take her to hear Lilli Lehman or Nellie Melba or Caruso? Now, wondering where they would put it, she imagined music she had not even thought about hearing in her lonely, isolated little sitting room.

She thought about it over the endless washing, pushing back a strand of hair with the back of her soapy hand, and the thought consoled her during the first sixteen hours alone with her three children, while father went to the hills for firewood. Gradually, throughout that winter, snatches of arias returned to her memory, and melodies she had forgotten during the past three years. Though she could not actually picture the gramophone father had ordered, that handicap did not trouble her. She never consciously tried to understand the difference between the old tube she had seen and the revolutionary discs the dealer at the Fort had described. At heart, she was an artist, untroubled by the mechanics of sound and reproduction.

She thought father had forgotten about the promise and the gramophone. Most evenings she watched him behind the weeks-old *Times* in the light of the bracket lamp, her hands busy with the mending that always accumulated faster than she could empty the bulging basket. Weeks after Christmas, one evening when she was washing the milk pail and covering the flat pans of still warm milk, she saw him go into our bedroom for what she expected would be the usual monotonous reading of *The Water Babies*. Instead he seemed to be telling us a story. Then she heard him singing. Incredulous, as she dried her hands she heard the rollicking tune and words from *Pinafore*:

> I polished all the brasses so carefully,
> And now I am the ruler of the queen's navee . . .

It was a scene she had never expected to see, Nora and me sitting up in bed in our sleepers, wide-eyed as we watched father do what she always did — sing to us. Still wiping her hands, she stood listening by the doorway, and when he realized she was there, he reached back to her. As though they had recently rehearsed it, together they sang the gay, amusing chorus and then repeated it.

They both seemed surprised that we did not want to go to sleep when they turned out the light and went back to the sitting room with one of those special looks that always made them happy. It was only after several appeals for a drink of water, and the perennial "I want to wee wee, mamma!" that father, in the voice we very well understood, firmly warned us to go to sleep or else!

The gramophone did not come that winter, nor did father mention it. Probably mother did not think about it either during the busy spring-time months of 1907. Without Leo's help, father worked on the land from dawn to dusk, pausing only to plough and disc the vegetable garden, leaving planting and weeding to mother in her spare moments between caring for their three children, doing the essential housework, and preparing meals. It was only during their brief meals together that she realized how fully his mind was occupied with the prospect of acquiring the legal recognition that marked his first great milestone as a farmer. Without his frequent voluble reminders she might have forgotten that this was the third anniversary of their arrival at the little knoll on the northwest quarter of Section 12 in Township 25, Range 14 west of the second meridian.

Soon after dawn on the eighth of June, she wished him well and watched him drive off to the booming little village of Lipton, ten miles north of the Fort, the village that justified the hopes expressed by the first settler she had met on that long, unforgettable ride behind the oxen. With the horses, father would be home from Lipton before dark, full of details about his visit to the new Dominion Lands Office with his formal application for a "patent to this homestead under the provisions of the Dominion Lands Act." Of course, he would sign his sworn statement as a "British subject by birth and always."

He had completed the terms of the agreement. He had built a log house whose recorded value of $120 was in line with the two cents a pound they had been offered for their prize onions and the sixty-five cents a bushel he had received for his first bags of wheat. The timbers had cost only his own and his brother's labor, and with their labor they had built the house. He had built a stable and a barn and dug the well; together they were valued at $400, more than three times the value placed on the house. He had twenty-eight acres ploughed and eight acres fenced. His family, according to the sworn statement, consisted of himself and his wife and their three children, and they had lived on the land continuously for the required three years, "So help me, God."

The duly signed document went on from the local agent to Ottawa on the eleventh of July. In the slow process of His Majesty's mail in 1907, almost two months passed before father received his patent duly "accepted as sufficient." The date was August 7.

A Ulyssean
Settler
and His Wife

The modest, limited Herd Law had whetted father's natural appetite for public service. The community needed roads and schools and local government. They needed literally every civilized amenity that in long-settled parts of the world had evolved over centuries of slow, struggling progress and trial and error, but above all they needed means of communication and transportation.

There was the C.P.R., linking older Eastern Canada and the Atlantic ports with Vancouver and the Pacific. There were a few trails, such as the Touchwood and tracks leading north from the Western States. Together they were the vital arteries, in many cases a hundred slow miles, or more, from most of the settlers' new log or sod shacks. Most of the trails, like the Touchwood now so familiar to father, were adequate for carts and oxen. Even then, they had provoked more profanity in more languages than the variety of ethnic origins of the men who cursed and used them. Most were worse than useless for horses.

Like the entire Carlton route linking the railway and the Qu'Appelle Valley with the North Saskatchewan River, the Touchwood Trail had just happened without benefit of surveyors, decades before the settlers arrived with their families.

With mother's eager approval father invited several of those settlers to a meeting at our geographically central house to discuss the concern that she knew must be uppermost in the thoughts of every woman in the scattered community, as well as the men's — roads. John George, the "old countryman" whose English wife soon became mother's best friend, talked about their desperate need for roads sufficiently improved to enable them to haul loads of grain to the elevators when the market was good, no matter what the weather. John Parker, later our member of parliament and speaker of the provincial legislature, stressed the need for some form of local government. But it was father who voiced mother's most anxious longing; for the means to get help quickly in case another prairie fire should threaten any one of them.

"Frost," he recalled later, "can kill a man's crop before maturity;

hail drive it into the ground; grasshoppers (they came later) eat what is left, but a prairie fire can dispossess us of it all. It was our most dreaded danger."

Whether it was that reference to the dread of fire or whether it was mother's hospitable cup of tea that followed the formal talk, the little group of men organized themselves into a committee with authority to look into every aspect of their situation. Above all, they were to investigate the difficult problem of financing the enormous amount of work involved. Before they left, with mother's invitation to bring their wives with them next time, they had made plans to tackle the roads first and had agreed on a levy of three dollars a quarter section.

Though mother naturally wondered where they would get even the three dollars required — they were perennially short of funds — she quickly forgot that concern in her joyous relief that help was coming at last. Whatever the cost, it was as nothing compared with the prospect of being able to visit a neighbor in a few hours, or to send for help in case of illness or an accident — such as had happened to father on that first logging trip with the horses — for the hope, no matter how remote, of closer contacts with civilization by way of the Fort. In the lovely euphoria of the gathering, she had not realized that father would be the logical choice for secretary-treasurer of the local improvement organization, nor that he would happily accept the responsibility.

The first operations were entirely local, but they marked the initial step toward a planned transportation system that would link the community not only with market centers but also with neighbors and the outside world that so often seemed hauntingly remote. That was the vision. In reality it was sheer hard, mucky labor for every man who had filed on his quarter section.

Homesteaders with horses — usually four-horse teams contributed by two neighbors — handled the primitive metal slush scrapers purchased with the first modest funds in a simple process of borrow and fill, loosening dirt from hills to level depressions. Men without teams cleared brush and trees from each stretch of roadway selected for improvement, often no more than a few yards ahead of the four-horse teams. For them all the great bonus, apart from the passable road, was the rare camaraderie of working together and the midday breaks for their meal of cold tea and bannock or sandwiches. After the ten-hour day, every man returned home to his regular chores that had commenced before dawn.

During the first couple of years some men worked out their taxes at statutory labor on the road allowance adjacent to their own land, an arrangement that too often resulted in neglect or poor grading. Eventually, after making a survey of the situation, the secretary-treasurer suggested that larger work gangs under experienced road bosses would ensure better roads and better use of their limited funds. The committee, aware that they must stretch their finances to construct some three hundred miles of north and south roads and make the cross roads passable, unanimously agreed to depute father to seek the estimated funds by way of a formal bond issue.

It was a commission to father's liking, though less so to mother's. Again she was faced with the prospect of spending days and nights without him, dependant on the kind help of their generous neighbor, Locktie. She accepted the situation only after he had painstakingly stressed the advantages of the road work to themselves as well as to the community. But she was not happy with it, nor was she able to share as enthusiastically as he would have liked his homecoming report: not only had he succeeded in his mission, but he had taken steps to organize their community into the Rural Municipality of Kelross.

Father, in his diplomatic way, further reassured her with news of a new railway line, the Grand Trunk, that would come within twelve miles of our farm, with a new town, LeRoss (the spelling was later changed to Leross), to be named for one of the railway company directors. They had chosen the site as the point at which to commence the now assured major road work. Inspecting the road makers' camp, with tents for the men and a cook, stabling for horses, and splendid equipment such as they had not dreamed of in the early stages of their progress as a community, took him away from home for several days at a time. Listening for the sound of his horses as she worked in the garden until the swift, shortening late-summer dusk, there were increasingly frequent moments when mother wondered whether she had ever lived in the warm, close proximity of family and friends in London.

But the road work was successful beyond their hopes, father was able to tell her eventually. They had actually set a cost of nine cents a cubic yard of fill that was to become the standard for several years.

Within two years the Rural Municipality of Kelross had progressed sufficiently for the election of a reeve and councillors. John George became the first reeve and father accepted the post of secretary-treasurer with a modest stipend. A small false-fronted frame municipal office followed the erection of the first grain elevator, and mother had the relief of seeing the records that had taken so much needed space in her sitting room removed to safer keeping in a shiny new iron safe.

During that momentous summer and the following winter when all the plans for the road work commenced, mother had been too pressed with the responsibilities she often had to manage alone. She had not been able to realize how much her husband was contributing to the immediate and more remote future of the community. As a result she had been completely unprepared for a generous compliment to him from John Locktie.

Locktie warmly praised father for his numerous achievements: plans for the road work; organization of finances that had seemed hopeless; organization and plans for municipal status.

He was having supper with them one evening after father had returned from a meeting with Mr. George, and he turned to mother: did she realize what a famous man her husband was becoming, how word of his versatility was spreading?

The scholarly neighbor raised his tea cup formally toward father and then to mother.

"Wilkins," he said, "like Ulysses is the perfect settler." He was a man who could cope with every new situation, and Mrs. Wilkins must be very proud of him.

Mother thanked him, raising her own cup to father. But there was a barely perceptible edge to her voice as she spoke, a note that father had not heard for years.

He remembered it a few days later when the newly engaged road boss drove up and delivered several great road scrapers, Johnston Bars, equipment that was to be stored in our yard. There was no mistaking the bitterness in her voice when she protested that they were a greater eyesore than the sod stable.

Father admitted, many years later, that the sudden sharp bitterness reminded him of the occasion when she had refused to marry him. He also recognized the strong undercurrent of emotion and something of her youthful determination.

They were standing in the yard, the road boss, father, and mother. The great wheeled equipment had been unloaded. The men talked about the advantages of scrapers that could move half a cubic yard of fill in half the time required by the hand scrapers they had been using. Father looked at those new scrapers lined up in two neat rows. Then he looked at the sod stable he knew mother had always loathed. Would she invite the road boss for dinner if he could persuade him to stay for the afternoon? If she would, he proposed that together, with one of those modern devices and the horses, they could demolish the stable well before supper time.

Her joy at the prospect was so obvious that he enjoyed recalling the occasion.

"We might have kept the old stable as a monument to our endeavor, but we were still too close to its back-ache memories to regard it with much affection or veneration. It must go to make room for something more pleasing, if only a patch of grass.

"I felt a certain sadistic joy at the prospect of doing away with that emblem of hard work as quickly as possible."

The sod walls, so arduously piled up row on row, crumpled and were removed to the nearest slough as fill for an extension of the vegetable garden. While mother watched from the back door, the two men cleared away the last remnants of sod. Suddenly the dog barked and the team of horses backed. The powerful Johnston Bar slipped, striking father across the chest and hurling him several feet from the remaining debris.

Mother's scream could have been heard for a mile. With his first slight movement, she was on her knees beside him as the road boss gently opened the blood-stained shirt and singlet, exposing the great gash.

In the usual pioneer way, they bathed and dressed the terrible wound as he recovered his breath, and applied bandages. Laconically, father summed up this latest fortunate escape:

"Had the bar struck my head the situation might have been worse — or better, depending on the point of view."

For the only time in those four years since she had seen the sod stable laboriously rise to its ugly roof, mother wished they had never tried to demolish it. Months later she wished fervently that she had never seen the scrapers either.

On a crisp, bright winter day, after a blanket of soft snow had turned the yard into a place of rare beauty, she took Nora and me out to play one of our favorite games, horses and driver; she was the driver, we were her team. Prancing up and down between the two rows of metal scrapers, Nora suddenly decided to copy a horse licking up snow for a drink. The metal was icy cold. Her tongue was warm and moist, and it stuck fast. Terrified, I pulled her away, leaving the tender skin frozen to the scraper. For weeks the poor child lived on bread softened in tepid milk.

Having savored the more diverting side of pioneer farming — he already realized that he would have preferred a life as a gentleman farmer — the Ulyssean settler had only one defense against the offer of an appointment as a local justice of the peace, his wife. Mother was not now quite as naive as she had been when he took on the Herd Law and responsibility for getting the road work underway. Torn by her instinctive wish not to discourage anything which might please him, she had to remind him that as a justice of the peace he would have to spend more time away from home. Father, doubtless anticipating so reasonable an objection, had his counter arguments ready: his duty as a citizen to help to maintain the law, if only for the protection of his family; the modest, and necessary, stipend that would go with the appointment; the fact that theirs was a quiet, law-abiding community which would make few demands on his services. To cap his arguments he alluded to the honor inherent in such an appointment; she was well aware of the prestige that went with an appointment as a justice of the peace in England. He even teased her about a share in the reflected glory.

Of course, mother eventually agreed that it was his duty to accept the appointment, as usual silently hoping that it would involve no more time or effort than he had suggested.

Within months of his acceptance she began to feel that her instinctive first reaction had been right. The strange burning of several neighbors' haystacks, clearly suggesting arson, involved countless hours of contact with the nearest detachment of the Royal Canadian North West Police, followed by the trial of the miscreant. Father must have had to exercise his finest ethical judgment as the charged man stood before him, a disgruntled bachelor who refused to pay the new school tax on the grounds that he had no children to be educated. During that entire case — it was dismissed — mother had been apprehensive of father's safety, daily dreading that some violence might occur.

But most of the numerous calls on his official time required no more than time, tact, and common sense and one provided a solution to a problem that was concerning both mother and himself. Together with the reeve, he was invited to a Ukrainian wedding.

Seated on trestles near the head of the long gaily decorated table set up in the barn, the two visiting gentlemen were invited to drink a special toast from a bottle being passed around the entire company. Father watched the reeve upend the bottle, somewhat surprised to note that his colleague securely corked the bottle with his tongue as he appreciatively gurgled. When father's turn came, he disregarded what apparently had been a warning. He took a good swig from the contents.

"One good swallow and involuntarily the muscles of my throat took charge of the situation," he told mother later. The concoction of homemade alcohol and raisins was sheer "liquid fire." To the extreme embarrassment of the justice of the peace, that generous swallow shot out across the table and sent the guest rushing out of doors in a violent attack of coughing that for minutes he could not control. At home, when the event had become merely an anecdote, he suddenly turned it to good use. It provided the solution to the problem that had been challenging his Yorkshireman's distaste for waste — what to do with an enormous crop of rhubarb.

During the spring following receipt of his patent, the rhubarb seed from that early package of onion seed had provided mother with the makings of so many deep pies that they never wanted to see another. The stalks grew tall and crisp and lusciously red and juicy, and he could not bring himself to cut them down for mulch. Remembering the raisin brew, one day he reached for the copy of *Enquire Within* in search of instructions for making wine. On his next trip to the Fort, he purchased the necessary vat and at the hotel bar obtained a couple of empty wooden casks. He and mother washed the rhubarb, cut and piled it into the vat, adding the necessary sugar and other ingredients according to the recipe in the invaluable volume. Months later, they carefully decanted what they hoped would be a drinkable wine, and bottled it. Late in the autumn, they opened a bottle.

It was clear when they held it up to the light. The bouquet pleased father as much as the dandelion wine he had enjoyed in Yorkshire. He offered a glass to the dour Scotsman Jock who with his wife Maggie had spent the summer in the tent, helping out when the combined duties of secretary-treasurer and justice of the peace had left father too little time for his own duties and mother too much time alone.

Jock and Maggie seemed to consider the wine a bit mild, frankly preferring, as they admitted, their more familiar Highland whiskey. They soon respected its potency, to mother's and father's amusement.

"Not an hour later Maggie was talking her head off and Jock had become almost as loquacious. They were both so merry it was almost impossible to get them to go to bed."

The contacts forced on him by his various official duties encouraged father to understand and respect many of the old-world customs with which he came in close contact during his pioneer years, customs as dear to the various ethnic groups as his English ways were to him. They were experiences that he often shared to our profit and occasionally to mother's amazement.

On one long winter drive on assessment duties in a small Slav community, he stopped at a prosperous looking house where he asked for food for himself and water for his horses. He was warmly welcomed and invited to a place at the long table covered with a clean white cloth and set neatly with plain crockery and cutlery. It was all just as he had experienced at several other pioneer homes until, to his amazement, his hostess reached under the bed across the room and brought out a metal box containing a round loaf of bread and some meat. Startled by the use of such unorthodox storage space, his tact barely survived when she again reached under the bed.

"This time she produced a handled bit of crockery not at all rare in rural bedrooms at the beginning of the century and from it produced a large pat of butter.

"Just how I adjusted myself to the circumstances without committing grave errors of misunderstanding between representatives of British-born and foreign-born Canadians, I do not quite know. To have remonstrated openly or to have refused the food would have been an unpardonable breach of hospitality. Besides my horses needed the rest and feed."

But the man who could cope with every situation in the rural municipality he loyally regarded as his personal responsibility, faced odds that often seemed insurmountable at home. Mother was in the fifth month of her fourth pregnancy and his duties during the coming summer threatened to take him away more than ever. There were days when he felt he must choose between leaving her alone and the pressure of road building; occasionally her eagerness for news about his day as they ate their late supper reminded him of how alone and isolated she must feel. Yet there was nothing he could do to change the situation; he felt he could not spend his entire time working his farm.

Fortunately his good fortune held. Conscience stricken — guilt was not his favorite word — he had sensed a perfect solution for them both when at the Fort he had heard about Jock and Maggie.

The middle-aged Scotch couple were looking for a place where they could spend the summer and see Western Canadian farm life at firsthand, hoping eventually to emigrate. Father explained that he could pay them nothing, but that they could have the tent for the summer and share the family table. To his delight, they accepted his offer; they liked him as much as they seemed to suit his needs. When he drove into the home yard, Maggie sat on the seat beside him and Jock on their luggage at the back. He had found a woman who would help mother in the house and a man to take over the chores and some of the farm work while he tended the affairs of the Rural Municipality of Kelross.

It was a good summer for all concerned. Mother seemed to prove the old Lowland Scots belief that some women are never happier or in better health than when they are pregnant. Some days, glancing in the mirror above the wash basin, she could not miss the fact that she looked almost as pretty as when she left home. Her coppery, dark hair had regained its luster, and when she trimmed her fringe it curled becomingly over her forehead.

I can remember little about it beyond her happiness. Though Nora and I were too young to understand anything about having a baby other than her obviously changed body, there was something between her and father that was more than a memory that has never faded. There was something special about his pat on her shoulder as she sat in the rocking chair or his quiet kiss on the nape of her neck as she stirred a pot of soup on the stove; about her smile when he came in for dinner with bits of news — the lark he had seen fighting off a predatory crow, or a new settler who had passed up the trail with his oxen, "just as we did."

It was the first of September when Mrs. McPherson came again, and the baby arrived the next day; that was when father commenced to talk about his girls, for again he did not have a son who eventually would help him on the farm and some day succeed him.

She was, as Mrs. McPherson said, "a bonnie wee bairn," healthy and with a sunny disposition that reflected mother's mood during a relatively happy pregnancy. They called her Dorothy Hildegard, Dodie for short, just as Sylvia had fondly become Sybbie and almost from that time father's little helper, as though he hoped his fair-haired third daughter would take the place of the non-existent son.

With Maggie's help, mother enjoyed her first rest since she had stepped down to the station platform at South Qu'Appelle. She continued to curl her fringe and to brush her hair until it shone and regained its natural little tendrils about the nape of her neck. When Mrs. McPherson allowed her to leave her bed, she put on the slim cotton frock she had made with the skirt that covered her ankles but did not gather dust from the floor. She bathed and dressed the baby and encouraged

Nora and me to fondle her, and even to hold her in our short, plump arms, a trust I carefully honored by not dropping her as I had dropped Sylvia.

There were no baptismal services for Sylvia and Dorothy, not because formal religion had yet to be introduced to our pioneer community. Nor had there been for the two of us born in London, possibly as a result of a decision reached between our parents before I arrived. Through most of his younger adult years father had attended many lectures sponsored by the contemporary free-thinking Fabian Society of moderate socialists whose members included H. G. Wells, Bernard Shaw, and the Webbs. He had also shared mother's interest in the small group of Cambridge undergraduates whose preference for contemporary modern church music was attracting attention.

She had been a chapel-goer with a relatively informed liking for the fine chapel music then at its splendid best in England. Father, despite his comparatively orthodox upbringing, had rebelled against the efforts of the overly zealous missionaries he had observed in Africa and their tendency to deprive primitive black men and women of their ancient guiding rituals without providing others they could understand and adapt to their ways of life. Whether for these reasons, or others, our parents had decided that baptismal vows as binding and significant as were then required by the Church of England should not be entrusted to proxies or surrogates. They should wait until we were old enough to make our own decisions, until we had learned to be aware of and to respect the laws of nature and family and, perhaps, of the universe. Father, particularly, had some lofty ideals to support his fine ideas.

The presence of the *Kyrie* was much more than a casual hanging of a beloved picture.

Mrs. McPherson had gone back to her own home a couple of weeks earlier, and Jock and Maggie were to leave before cold weather forced them out of the tent. Father had taken his harvest in, and mother returned to her usual household duties. Life was back to normal, it seemed, when he came home from LeRoss and told her about meeting the reeve and the neighbor who was considered a likely chairman of the proposed school board. They had talked about raising funds to build the school and unanimously again father was nominated to negotiate the necessary debentures; this time he would have to go to Winnipeg.

Mother asked when he expected to go to Winnipeg, and for how long, her voice very quiet. In his enthusiasm over the project he failed to detect an echo of the sharpness that had alerted him the day he had been toasted as the Ulyssean settler. Reaching for his pipe — it was the after-meal hour when most of the family discussions occurred — he replied that it would probably be toward the end of October or early in

November, when the autumn work was over. And it would only be for ten days or so.

Instead of the shared enthusiasm he, as usual, had expected, something in her response made him lay down his pipe.

Had he forgotten, she asked, that Maggie and Jock were leaving at the end of October?

It was a response that he had actually anticipated, and he hastened to tell her that he had already spoken to John Locktie, again asking him to come over daily to look after the chores. Locktie, of course, had willingly agreed, and he would get through them much more quickly than Jock ever did.

For a moment her steady gaze held him. For a second time her look reminded him of the young woman who had flatly refused to go to Africa as his bride. In the same disturbingly quiet voice she asked him if he expected her to stay alone with four small children, the youngest not yet two months old; even if Mr. Locktie did come over twice a day, who would look after those children if she took ill or fell down the cellar steps again or if there was another prairie fire?

Father's only answer was to assure her that no such emergencies would occur; that she was needlessly imagining trouble; crossing bridges unnecessarily. He had been so delighted with the prospect of the trip and its significance that he had assumed that she would share what amounted to a sort of family honor. She wanted a school as keenly as he did, and without funds no school would be built. Besides, it was up to them to make their contribution to the progress of the municipality.

His arguments fell on the ears of a woman who, though she had not consciously faced the ages-old decision, had chosen between her man and what she considered to be their children's welfare. Mother flatly refused to stay alone.

To him his situation seemed much more difficult than hers. Though he had tried to adapt to the needs and the demands of a wife and a family, all of whom he truly loved, he believed in his duty to his community as clearly as he felt entitled to that trip to Winnipeg and a man's right to an occasional break from domesticity. Whether through stubbornness or determination, he would find a way and, as so often happened, he found it easily: Jock and Maggie had no objection to staying on for another couple of weeks, though they would have to move their camp beds into the sitting room because the nights were getting too cold to sleep in the tent.

Mother watched him drive out of the yard with his load of grain, on his way to South Qu'Appelle and the train to Winnipeg, with less than warmth. She knew he had been disturbed by her attitude, but for that she felt no regret; he might have consulted her before accepting the duty; he must also realize that it was not right to leave so many young children alone with her for what might well be two entire weeks.

Yet when the wagon and team disappeared beyond the bluff near the turn into the Touchwood Trail she wondered if she had been unreasonable. Other settlers left their families alone. Other wives accepted loneliness and anxieties. She began to feel that she was not the proper wife for such a Ulyssean settler as John Locktie had suggested. As the days and nights passed she wanted her husband almost as ardently as she had wanted him that night more than four years ago when he tramped off alone to inspect their new farmsite. Not even Maggie's endless talk and all the needs of the children hastened the days until he came home again.

He was very glad to be home. That was evident as soon as he jumped down from the wagon. Eager to tell her about everything that had happened, he clearly exuded pride in the success of his undertaking. Of course, the new school would be built, though he still could not tell her exactly where. As Jock looked after the horses and helped to carry in the Gladstone bag and the parcels and boxes, they had both forgotten the differences that had disturbed them both before his departure.

No one, including father, wanted to wait until after supper to open the parcels, but on that mother was firm; supper, and then they would clear the table.

There were woollen mitts for Maggie and socks for Jock; toys for us children and other parcels that, father said, would be opened only at Christmas. Not until Jock and Maggie had gone to bed, in our west bedroom temporarily, was mother alone with father and then she opened her own present.

All evening, ever since he had reached into his bulging Gladstone bag and held up the parcel in its tissue paper, she had wondered what he had brought her: woollen underthings, she hoped and expected; she sorely needed warm chemises and petticoats to replace those she had brought with her from home; woollen stockings or carpet slippers.

Carefully she opened the first real present her husband had bought her since leaving London, her hands all thumbs as she untied the ribbon knots and spread the tissue on the table. Instead of warm woollen garments her chilblained fingers lifted a dress length of exquisite white chiffon, delicately embroidered with designs in violet silk thread.

In London she could have worn a gown such as the material suggested to a Lord Mayor's reception or a gala at Drury Lane or Covent Garden; it must surely have been one of the very few such dress lengths available in Winnipeg, much as his brief comments indicated that the city had grown and improved.

Between tears and laughter she buried her face against his shoulder, hoping the soft lamp light concealed her immediate reaction until she could muster words of appreciation; telling herself that not every prairie settler gave his wife lovely embroidered chiffon. I know how she felt because on one of my birthdays he bought me a pair of white boots when

I had only black stockings and dared not risk wearing them in the dust, or mud, that surrounded the house.

Carefully she rewrapped the delicate fabric, talking excitedly about the gown she would some day make, and led him off to bed, a wise woman who knew that there were more ways for a man to express his love than in his impractical choice of a gift.

Tomorrow, he could tell her more about the arrangements he had made in Winnipeg and accept the congratulations of the reeve and councillors on behalf of the Rural Municipality of Kelross. Tonight, that dear, lordly, unpredictable husband was hers.

The Stars
Are Shining

Sometimes she wished she were like some of the other settlers' wives — physically strong, much more adaptable, in every way better suited to her new life. Yet actually, she knew very few of them. Mrs. George and Mrs. Parker were her friends, and she knew what they were like. She had visited them in their homes, perhaps half a dozen times with each. She had been to Mrs. Kamerer's, and despite the handicap of her lack of German and Mrs. Kamerer's still inadequate English, their common interests bridged many a rueful, stilted discussion about their children's ailments or firewood so green that no effort could get an oven hot enough to bake an acceptable batch of bread. They had all been at her house. It never occurred to her to wish that she was like them, or to want them to be like her. It was the women she had never met whose lives filled many of her lonely thoughts.

They were dream women. Figments of her imagination. Images built up from father's comments about those he had met or had described to him. They were women living fifteen or twenty miles away, immigrants from her own old country and European lands, or Americans who she thought of as being like Mrs. Parker, out-going, friendly, accustomed to prairie life. They were women who knew how to make the crisp, tasty, delicious ginger cookies that we children begged her to bake for us, but they were never whole women whom she could see in their own surroundings.

Because father talked so much about local events that constituted part of the developing province, she pictured them as being far more numerous than they were. Though between 1901 and 1911 the population had increased from one hundred thousand to five hundred thousand, the vastness of the prairies and the new towns erupting along the new railway branches as well as the C.P.R. main line easily absorbed them all. Had she known how few and far between those homesteads were, her own house would have seemed as small as a thimble on Hampstead Heath.

She did not envy the woman who stored the butter in a chamber pot under the bed. Nor the Doukhobors father described — hardy, intensely religious women in the commune near Yorkton who hitched themselves tandem to a single plough while one of their men guided the blade deep into a new furrow. She would not exchange her life for that of any woman living in the new Orthodox Jewish settlement near Lipton where they still honored the ancient biblical custom of living apart during menstruation and after childbirth.

But she did envy one aspect of life among the gay, partnering Ukrainians, the women who casually loaded a couple of water barrels on a stoneboat, hauling the family's supply from the nearest slough, driving the team of horses or the yoke of oxen they had harnessed. She longed to hear their melodic, patriotic songs that linked them with the homeland the first Canadian generation would never forget. Those songs she could understand and appreciate as she could never appreciate their intense satisfaction with homesteading, with the opportunity merely to work patiently and tirelessly. Nothing in her limited experience enabled her to realize the extent to which for them the New World meant an end to grinding poverty and serfdom, or to some, an end to the constant fear of actual slavery. This was their land of freedom as well as of opportunity. It promised hope and a modest fortune for their children.

For her children she wanted much more, and not merely because of the intellectual snobbishness of the class from which she had come. She never forgot that this great Western Canada would need more than a single generation to achieve a fulfilling, lasting civilization of its own, that the vaunted Western Canadian optimism had its limitations, and that like a mirage it must have something real to reflect against the dawn mists of a summer morning.

One woman whom she partly envied, and never met, was Miss Georgina Binnie-Clark, the English Rodean graduate who had already established her own well-equipped place south of the Qu'Appelle Valley. Though like all women Miss Binnie-Clark was denied the masculine privilege of filing on land for the modest fee of ten dollars, her drudgery had been eased by regular and generous remittances from home. Her house was completed with surrounding verandahs. Her stables and granaries were also finished.

Binning, from all father had heard about the farm, was modern in every way from its equipment and horses to its management. Its mistress prided herself on being able to manage it herself, and to pitch hay, drive her own harrows, and do her own seeding and stooking and harvesting. She needed no masculine help — and apparently little masculine advice, according to father — other than a couple of farm hands. It was not this vaunted independence that mother liked; she was inclined to agree with father that Miss Binnie-Clark might be one of those modern feminist women; but like the other wealthy group at Cannington, south of the railway, she was not a real pioneer, and it was that aspect of her life that mother tended to envy.

The Cannington people interested mother and she thought about them when the drudgery of her own life threatened to overwhelm her. Cannington Manor had become a western tradition of sorts by the time father filed on his quarter section. Its stables were huge and well equipped, as were the granaries and, as every newcomer soon heard, so was its great house, all set down on the bald prairie. Its owner had imported riding horses and he and his guests, attired in traditional faded hunting pink, rode to hounds as though they were still in their English countryside. Mother, who had never ridden a horse, naturally compared racing across the prairie to a ploughman's slow, steady gait. She found it difficult to share father's opinion, and that of the few neighbors she met, that such extravagant innovations would do little to advance settlement, or the argument that this particular colony had little need for gentlemen farmers who might better get on with a bit more ploughing.

She felt a surge of sympathy when the Cannington people sold their hounds and thoroughbred horses — settlers with less capital insisted that they had been forced to sell — and the brief exciting era of fox-hunting disappeared, perhaps forever, from Saskatchewan. For her the attempt at mildly gracious living was as understandable as father's approval of their contribution to raising the standard of prairie horses. Like the community founded to the southeast of us by the Hungarian Count Esterhazy, the prairies needed the leaven of such bizarre experiments.

In many ways, these communities were no more incongruous than the bachelors who filed on their quarter sections and built their log or sod shelters with unrealizing abandon miles from one another and the nearest neighbor, many of them, also, with hopes and ambitions far beyond their modest capital. A few of the bachelors depended on regular remittances from families in the older countries. But whether with or without support beyond their own endeavors, they all became familiar figures at every primitive schoolhouse dance or box social, eager to meet the rare unattached girl who paid a visit to homesteading relatives.

Father's descriptions of the prairie bachelors, heard on his municipal duties, provided mother with other glimpses of life somewhere beyond her own immediate poplar bluffs and sloughs. One young man he met when he called to explain local assessment charges was not unique. Whoa-ing his oxen at the end of a long furrow on a narrow field, he offered father tobacco and settled back, leaning against the handle of his plough. Instead of the usual farmer's attire of denim overalls, he wore trousers that obviously belonged to formal evening dress and a dress shirt minus collar and white tie. He explained that he had been to a dance "in town," got home at dawn, and decided to get on with his ploughing while the day was yet cool.

But while some settlers arrived, others left, among them the Jonas family with whom our parents had spent occasional visits which they had hoped to continue. Lacking the peculiar vision of men like father, for Mr.

Jonas life was too brief to spend trudging behind a plough or pitchforking manure from a primitive stable. He and his wife were among the thousands of immigrants who within a few years again became emigrants, people who, with the slightest encouragement from father, mother often gladly would have followed.

Yet she did not want to change places with any of those women, except perhaps on occasions such as the raging November blizzard that kept us all indoors.

The weather was too treacherous for father to risk taking out the team, and for four days he never left the house except to do essential chores and bring in wood and the snow mother melted. He hated the clothesline strung across the sitting room and the smell of wet woollens drying in front of the open oven. He complained about the noise we children made and threatened to shut us into their bedroom; he even made and hung a door for the purpose. His irritation troubled mother and in turn the baby she was still nursing. If the wind had continued to buffet the house and patches of blue sky had not showed through the curtain of heavy snow, none of us might have survived the awful tension.

It was always that way on the farm. We children grew up accustomed to recurrent storms and fair weather and the effects the changes had on our parents. That evening, after the storm had subsided, mother quietly walked up and down the sitting room, untroubled by the clotheslines, gently cradling Dodie and massaging her straight little back to release the last bubble of gas before putting her to sleep in her crib. Father sat near the bracket lamp, reading his weeks-old copy of the *Times,* the light silhouetting the outline of his Van Dyke beard. When she sat down across the table from him and reached for her mending basket, he put down the paper.

That must be her favorite song, he remarked, the *Tosca* aria she had been crooning as she nursed the baby. He had heard her sing it often to the children and it seemed to be specially right tonight, now that the stars were shining. It reminded him, he said, as he looked at the calendar on the wall, that he must go to the Fort next week.

But why, she wondered, did "The Stars Are Shining" remind him to go to the Fort? And in December when he could buy any of the things they needed at the new store in LeRoss or ask Mr. Locktie to do any of his errands when he went to the Fort with his last load of grain? Besides, he knew she could not stay alone with the children.

But she would not be alone, he assured her. A few days ago, before the storm, he had asked their latest new neighbors to let one of their boys ride over on his horse each afternoon, do the chores, and sleep on the couch in the sitting room; she could not want for anyone more reliable than one of the Drew boys.

For a moment the evening's pleasant atmosphere threatened to return to the tensions of the past few days. Mother resented his arrangements made without consulting her. She felt he had no right to risk such a seemingly unnecessary trip. And she dreaded being alone, even for a few days and with the reliable help of the young neighbor. But something she could not explain, something in his manner when he mentioned her song, softened her protest.

As usual when he was going to the Fort, father left before daylight, and mother faced a long, lonely day with the weather still too cold to take Nora and Sybbie and me out to play. She was still tired from the strain of the storm, and she hesitated to leave Dodie alone in the house. Because she had seriously begun to worry about the lack of a school near enough for us to attend, she decided to amuse us with a game that we would never forget. It was a game that freed her from every vestige of envy she had felt about the physical stamina of other settlers' wives and their ability to help with farm work.

She sat us at the table and gave each of us a sheet of her precious letter-writing paper and a lead pencil. With the folding rule from father's tool box she drew lines on the paper. Then, to our wide-eyed expectancy, she made some marks on each page. Letters of the alphabet. We were going to learn how to write, and some day we would also read.

Father was back as he promised, just before supper, three days later. As soon as we heard the first sound of the sleigh bells, we children rushed to the window. Our hands and faces had been washed and our hair brushed. Mother had nursed the baby and tucked her into her crib. She had tidied her own hair and she glanced briefly into the looking glass over the wash basin as she hurried to open the door.

He came in, a great burst of cold air with him. Stamping to get the snow off his boots, he laid a pile of parcels on the floor, kissed her lightly on the tip of her nose and said he must look after the horses.

When he came in again, his arms were filled with more parcels, and with an air of mystery he told mother to clear the sturdy little table in the corner behind her rocking chair. The mystery deepened when he very carefully laid a huge, square parcel on the table. On his last trip out to the sleigh he carried in another parcel wrapped in brown paper, a large parcel with a very strange shape.

Of course we older children begged to know what was in the parcels, and mother looked very curious. To our every insistent enquiry he told us we must wait until he had done the chores and everyone had eaten.

We were all tired and hungry and excited and we did not realize that he, too, was very tired after his long round trip. When he came in from milking the cow and hung up his coat and fur cap, we clamored around him, usually a sign for a romp. We still failed to realize how tired and irritable he was when he told us that if we weren't quiet we would go to bed without our suppers. Turning to mother, he said we all needed a good spanking to make us behave — he had always maintained that spanking girls was her responsibility and that he would make up for it by giving his sons a jolly good hiding when they needed it. She was tired, too, and tense with the usual demands of a family waiting for supper. Somehow she got us to our chairs at the table and served the meal. The awful moment passed. We got into our sleepers while she washed up. Then, with the supper table completely cleared, father, rested and fed, asked her to bring the scissors and began to cut the strings on the largest parcel.

She should have known what it was, though she certainly gave no indication if she did. She was as excited as we children, watching every careful cut of the scissors, every unfolding sheet of paper. As the square, dark oak box emerged, she burst into tears. She rushed to him and threw her arms about him. And she told us what it was — a gramophone.

Carefully he settled it on the little table and adjusted the level. He dramatically opened the other large parcel, the huge bell-shaped horn of the E. Berliner model that had come from Montreal. It was one of the machines that were advertised in Canadian newspapers he had been shown at the Fort, variously priced from forty dollars to twice as much. He removed the tissue-paper wrappings from several small parcels and fitted each item into place. Finally, he opened a flat package we had not noticed in the excitement. From it he lifted five round black discs, three with red labels, and two with black labels. Gramophone records. Quietly and dramatically, he read the titles on the labels.

An excerpt from *Tannhäuser*, "The Evening Star"; we could look outside any evening, he told us children, and see such a star, and he said it as though he was easing mother's moment of overwhelming delight. The next title on a red seal record was Mimi's song from *La Bohème*, chosen from the limited selection available at the Fort, and two of her favorite arias from poignantly remembered London concerts at Drury Lane and Covent Garden.

In our sleepers and wrapped in blankets on the couch, Nora and I listened to our first gramophone record, the first music we ever heard. For us there was something prophetic in his choices, in that aria from *Tosca*, "The Stars Are Shining," sung by the tenor Enrico Caruso; mother explained that it was the farewell song of a young man for the lady he loved, sung from a dark, cruel prison. In some strange way, those arias symbolized a wonderful other light that shone on our seemingly narrow, illiterate little prairie world. They came to symbolize mother's dear, priceless contribution to our growing awareness. They were equally an expression of father's quixotic love that encompassed his dedication to the land as much as his gifts of the yards of white chiffon and one of the earliest gramophones in the district. He had remembered his year-old promise, that was the knowledge she cherished as she made her secret, impossible vow never to become cross with him again.

For Christmas Day they invited the George family and John Locktie for dinner "and some music." We had never shared the day with so many people, and it was a memorable event. Father had carefully chosen and hoarded the special roast of beef. Mother steamed the English plum pudding. We children, along with the young Georges, stuffed ourselves on chocolates and nuts and played games together. And late in the day, John Locktie made the comment that stamped it as unforgettable.

He stood in front of the door in his overshoes and coat and heavy woollen scarf. Fur cap in hand, he postponed as long as he could the moment when he must head out into the bitter cold wind and his two-mile walk across the drifted snow. He had repeated his thanks for the best Christmas dinner he had eaten since coming to Canada and again he referred happily to that wonderful music that reminded him of the wise words of one of his Scottish countrymen more than a century before.

"Give me the making of the songs of a people," he repeated, "and I care not who makes its laws."

Though Mrs. Wilkins did not make the songs they had enjoyed that afternoon, her interest in sharing them meant as much to the development of the new land as her husband's newly ploughed fields. He wished every settler and his family could have listened to Caruso as a Christmas present and, above all, to the deep, lovely voice of Madame Ernestine Schumann-Heink singing "The Holy City"; that gramophone and the recorded music that filled the house was truly a modern miracle. And then, pulling his cap down over his ears, as a swift, sudden burst of frigid air cut into the room, he was gone, his good-night echoing the farewells of the Georges who had left earlier because they had a long drive home.

At the time no one present could have imagined how far afield those songs would be remembered, nor for how long.

One winter many decades later, Nora and I were holidaying in Hawaii with members of the family. As a pleasant diversion after sun-drenched days on a Kihei beach, we listened to the regular P.B.S. broadcast from the mainland, rebroadcast from Honolulu. In a program from Lincoln Center in New York Luciano Pavarotti was to sing a group of tenor arias, including some from Verdi's *Tosca*. Suddenly, from across the room Nora and I turned to one another.

"That is one of my earliest memories," she said, echoing my own thought and my own emotion. It was "The Stars Are Shining" from act 3 that we had first heard on the couch beside the leopard skin in the log house father had built with his own hands.

It was an experience that had occurred many times before that evening in Hawaii, and since. More than half a century after we left the farm, listening to entire operas on acoustically perfect machines, I am not reminded of The Met, Massey Music Hall, Covent Garden, or La Scala. My mind goes back to those lovely, melodic songs mother sang to us or the tunes she crooned as she nursed her latest baby. Pavarotti becomes Enrico Caruso, though it was years after the arrival of the first gramophone that we were old enough to recognize either the name of the works we heard or those of the various performing artists.

Mother later arranged an evening of music for a few close neighbors, a *soirie* she laughingly called it, a typically wonderful, practical, artistic occasion. Knowing that she lacked the means as well as the energy to get her four children to bed and to provide or prepare a meal for the twelve or twenty guests who might be able to come, she offered only tea and coffee and suggested that they bring their own supper.

Of course they understood. And of course they all came. When we children, Wilkins and neighbors, were bedded down wherever there was a spare corner, father wound up the gramophone and cleared his throat, a self-chosen and very happy concert master.

I have no means of knowing the titles of the records he dusted and placed on the turntable that evening. All I know is that they included the few available at the local dealer's, now listed only in the earliest catalogues at prices then ranging from the $1.25 for the first one-sided short-playing instrumental "Air on the G String" by Bach to a $7.50 "Sextette" from *The Bride of Lammamoor*.

I can only begin to understand what that evening meant to each of those entertainment-starved pioneers before the emergence of radio and television and instant news coverage from around the world and beyond. I can only guess at the emotions of each man and woman crowded into the small, relatively well-lit, relatively warm room; just to be with other people and to share such an experience for a few hours was heaven on earth. But I have no hesitation in assuming that then and there, as with every occasion when a fortunate owner of a gramophone wound up his machine, someone — shyly or in a whisper hoarse with emotion — mentioned the title everyone seemed to know, "None But the Lonely Heart." Certainly no one would have considered such a comment a cliché.

Among the records that I know our parents had collected were that excerpt from *Tosca*; the Schumann-Heink; a "single side" *Carmen*; Mimi's tragic farewell aria from *La Bohème*; Bach's "Air on the G String"; something from Gilbert and Sullivan; and a gay medley of songs from *The Bohemian Girl*, another of mother's romantic favorites. She and father had listened to *The Bohemian Girl* more than once at Drury Lane and had paused to admire the statue of Balfe, its composer, in the glittering foyer. When he had replaced the last of the records in its envelope, father favored the guests with his unaccompanied rendering of "I Dreamt That I Dwelt in Marble Halls," and a rambling account of a performance of *Tannhäuser* that he illustrated with a copy of a program from one of the earlier productions.

To round out the evening, and before they linked arms and sang "Auld Lang Syne," he showed them his collection of photos of celebrities in the enamelled, book-shaped album — among them Ellen Terry, Mrs. Patrick Campbell, and Dan Leno. When every visiting child had been wakened and dressed, and every foot-warming stone had been retrieved from the oven or the top of the stove and heater, he banked the fires for what remained of the night. The log house returned to its own isolation.

Sadly, the neighbors who had shared in the evening left a souvenir that was to cloud its memory for weeks.

Though we had weathered other cold winters and had enjoyed many improvements since the sod roof nearly annihilated us all, we were unprotected against the effects of overcrowding with other children. We suffered our first epidemic of severe colds.

Day after day mother washed the handkerchiefs she soaked in a pail of water well laced with salt. The clothesline never came down, the oven door was never free of sleepers and diapers except when she baked batches of bread that failed to tempt the finicky appetites. Father developed one of the periodic aftermaths of the malaria that had kept him in a Beira hospital for six weeks, and for a couple of days was so desperately ill that when John Locktie delivered the weekly batch of mail, the good neighbor insisted on doing the chores until his fever and the malarial "shakes" subsided. Short of sleep because both Sybbie and Dodie suffered coughs she thought might be croup, in desperation one day mother allowed Nora and me to open her glove box.

I scarcely remember her admonition to be careful and put everything back where we found it because the recollection of opening the filagree silver clasp still seems like going into some far away, never-never land.

The fragrance of attar of roses lingered in the crystal vial from a Bond Street shop. On the satin-lined cover, a niche held the ivory glove stretchers. Below were several pairs of white kid gloves; to our "what do they say?" she answered from the kitchen that they were the cleaners' marks, once mundane but now nostalgic and to us romantic. We held the garnet earrings and the ring and wide garnet-encrusted bracelet in their opened boxes, companion pieces to the garnet-rimmed watch she sometimes wore pinned to the front of her blouse. Under them all lay the snub-nosed bullet that had saved father's life when his companion Johnstone felled the water buffalo; the tiny green-velvet box with the pearl engagement ring appealed more to our feminine instincts.

Father felt better that day and he paused in his wandering about the sitting room and picked up the ring. Looking across to mother bent over the scrub board he suggested that she put it on. When she shook her head and bent again to the washing, he took Sybbie on his knee and told us the story of the bit of gold he had bought from a dark-skinned man near the site of the fabled mine alleged to have belonged to the Queen of Sheba, and the pearls such as he had seen fished up from the Indian Ocean near Beira. Then he rambled on about the bazaar in Zanzibar where he had taken the gold and the pearls to the jeweller who made the ring.

His convalescence tried mother more than the worst hours of his illness. As he began to feel well enough to do his own chores, she hoped that getting out of the house would relieve his boredom. Instead, every hour he remained indoors he charged up and down the room like a caged lion. His temper flared with every childish tantrum. He scolded us unmercifully, and when mother tried to placate him he turned his quick anger on her.

She had been desperate when she ruled the sheets of paper and showed us how to make the letters of the alphabet. She was even more desperate that cold January day when she went to the what-not and picked up one of the African albums. Laying it on the table, she suggested that he might help to keep us quiet by showing us some of the photos he had taken.

The suggestion was a God-sent blessing. Grudgingly at first, he sat down and opened the album, casually turning page after page until he noticed a photo that reminded him of the day he had made it. Then he called to Nora and me to come and look at it.

That day the albums became our picture books. Gradually, we learned to recognize practically every great wild creature that inhabited the territory south of the Zambezi River, among them enormous boa constrictors grotesquely bloated with a recently engorged young buck. Ignoring the fact that we were still at kindergarten age, or oblivious of it, father illustrated those photos with trophies about the sitting room: the zebra whose tail was our fly swatter and that still hangs in my study, heavy rhinoceros tusks, and a sharp-toothed leopard's jaw bone. We learned about thatched Zulu houses and warriors and black mothers holding naked babies in their arms.

If there was any doubt about the authenticity of his yarns in our childish minds, he produced a letter that supported many of the claims, one he had written from Beira, Portuguese East Africa on September 3rd, 1896. It was addressed to "My dear Jos," his younger brother then in Johannesburg, Z.A.R.

"I cannot give you a detailed account of my adventures, but they were worthy of the name.

"I went off up the line with my camera and gun. And you would have liked to be along of me, old chap. I had a glorious time. Fell in with Johnstone at Bamboo Creek, went out to his camp about fifteen miles away, stopping there ten days.

"I had some grand sport and helped kill almost every kind of buck out there. Johnstone killed two lions while I was there and one day we got on to a herd of almost eighty buffaloes, wounding four of them and killed two and had the nearest squeak I ever had. I came back with one bull buffalo, one cow, one crocodile, one wildebeest, two hartebeest, and one Oribi horn. . . ."

Father told us about the narrow squeak.

He had set up his camera near a fine herd of water buffalo that Johnstone praised as the best he had seen in many years of game hunting. Carefully checking exposure and distance, father focussed his lens on a superb specimen, intent on getting a rare picture. With his black hood over his head, he had no thought for the potentially lethal power of the strongest of wild beasts. Suddenly, over his shoulder a shot rang out. Johnstone had dropped the water buffalo as it charged within yards of the fragile tripod and the unwary young photographer — our future father. It was the proof of that escape that lay under the treasures in mother's glove box. There was also the diary he had painstakingly kept during those three years in Africa, addressed to *My Dearest Nellie*.

Exhausted from nursing sick children and their ailing father, the last sound his Nellie wanted to hear was his droning voice recalling gruesome hunting expeditions. She was much more interested in seeing again his photos of the spires of Oxford seen through the mists; Kew and other famous gardens; the funeral of Queen Victoria; the coronation of King Edward VII who wore a beard just like father's; outings shared with mother on the Thames and captioned Boulter's Lock and Maiden Head and Windsor.

None of them interested us children more than the Frenographs, the special albums of family pictures. To children who had never seen gentlemen in white trousers and blazers and straw boaters, glimpses of them handing elegant ladies into punts was the kind of romance that belonged to fairy stories. We never tired of looking at the ladies' long skirts and white blouses with long sleeves and incredibly high collars, and at the straw hats perched on piled-up hair where they could never have stayed during a prairie wind. We were so impressed with the pretty blouses that one day mother opened one of the special boxes and showed us that once she had worn clothes such as she never wore now.

The album filled with pictures included one with me in her arms; another of her plump, bald infant in the *point d'esprit*-trimmed bassinet, wearing the embroidered and tucked robe that must have been a yard and a half long; a photo of Nora already looking somewhat like our Aunt Kate, mother's loveliest sister. Father was there in the reserve uniform of the Royal Engineers, ramrod straight, suitably moustached.

If mother ever felt that we might escape becoming some sort of monstrous little prodigies of learning, most of the books we had were equally as unusual for young children. Tom, Charles Kingsley's grimy little chimney-sweep water baby, was as far removed from our experience as Rudyard Kipling's Mowgli for whom we often nicknamed

Nora because she was such a tomboy. The Brothers Grimm peopled a world beyond our homestead with gnomes and ogres who fascinated us but had no connection with life around us. I can recall no parental objection to the fact that although I had read *The Secret Garden* before I was eleven, I had also read Marie Corelli's *Thelma* three times.

We carried in our young minds many pictures of Zulus and Matabele, but we knew nothing about the native Indians who sometimes stopped at our house in their buckboards, demanding tea with plenty of sugar in it; we had never been to the reserves between which they travelled from the Qu'Appelle Valley north to Nokomis or Punnichy. We knew more about England than about the province in which we lived. We knew the names of famous leaders such as Cecil Rhodes and old Kruger before we had heard of Sir Wilfrid Laurier or even Clifford Sifton, who, unwittingly, had played so important a part in our lives. We had heard about the Gilbert and Sullivan "Three Little Maids from School" before we began to wonder what a school might be. Mother sang "The Stars are Shining" when we had never heard either "O Canada" or "The Maple Leaf Forever" — or seen a maple tree.

We were just like other pioneer prairie children prior to 1910 or generally during the decade before the First World War: expatriates from a score of other lands, still clutching the memories our parents had brought with them.

None of us, and certainly none of our parents, realized how swiftly those other lives in other lands were about to be submerged by the exciting, technological future.

For us all the swiftest, more challenging changes came with the first Canadian newspapers and periodicals placed in our trail-side mail boxes by the man who carried the rural mail in his democrat or sleigh. Instead of the overseas edition of the London *Times,* Dante's *Inferno,* or H. G. Wells' dramatic *War of the Worlds,* father now spent his rare spare evening hours reading the *Regina Leader,* the *Manitoba Free Press,* and the saffron-jacketed *Farmer's Advocate* that was so nearly the color of ripe wheat, just like every other literate or semi-literate homesteader.

Lord
Have Mercy . . .

During the spring of 1909 mother silently wished that she could wholeheartedly share father's optimism. That she, too, could believe that at last they had overcome most of the hazards and hurdles of pioneering; accept his assurance that this year they were in for a bumper crop and all the fruits of the life he had chosen. Throughout May and June he talked about little else; above all the fine weather and fields that looked so splendidly promising, vindicating his belief in sowing only the finest seed he could buy. Evening after evening, in the short last light before sundown, she stood beside him surveying the largest wheat field he had ever planted, trying to catch his confident mood until she could lead him to talk about that other topic that meant almost as much to him, the new school. Eskdale School was due to be built on the first of July. He considered the choice of Dominion Day to be a good omen and a fitting celebration of his efforts to raise the necessary funds.

Yet there were times when even the promise of the school seemed too good to be true. After all the setbacks and disappointments they had shared, mother wished he would not be quite so sure that everything would prosper; that everything would go according to his plan. It seemed like courting bad luck. Better to hope than to be too sure, no matter how loyally she believed in his abilities.

For there was more to her concern than her thoughts of all the troubles they had survived, something she may never have discussed with him; something that I have come to appreciate because, along with at least one of my sisters, I have inherited it. Not actually premonition. A presentiment, possibly, or a tendency to have hunches that were born out too often to be completely ignored. Even father had come to recognize this quality in his wife, though when he referred to it, affectionately most of the time, it was usually to tease her about her weird north-country "weather vane." With his many generations of Yorkshire inheritance, his quiet teasing may have added a special bond between them.

Fortunately, mother's hunches occurred infrequently. On the first of July she had no time to think about anything except the early morning

preparations for the family's departure, repeatedly reminded by father
that the school had to be built and roofed before sundown.

She had packed a generous lunch basket, enough food for her own
family and for a bachelor or two who might turn up with only bannock
or days-old boiled beef. She had ironed our best, sadly outgrown frocks
and she wore one of her prettiest blouses and a long gay chiffon scarf
about her straw boater and her hair. Father held the baby while she
climbed into the buckboard. As usual he told us older children seated on
a blanket at the back to be quiet so that he could hear himself think.

His marvellously buoyant mood recalled the *Punch* joke he and
mother had laughed about, and that was utterly incongruous in such
glorious weather.

Of course she remembered it, he suggested. The typical soggy English
day and a typical Cockney family off to Kew. The husband trudging on
ahead, followed by his bedraggled wife, her rain-dampened hair clinging
to her wet cheeks, the baby in her arms and two slightly older children
tugging at her skirt. And the typically *Punch* caption, "I brought you out
to enjoy yerself, and you're jolly well going to!"

Nothing like that could occur in Canada, he remarked, flicking the
horses' reins. Not in weather like this; fresh air, plenty of space, and
instead of soggy Kew Gardens, the entire prairie and the prospect of a
new school.

For him the day lacked nothing.

"Everyone for miles around came to assist whether he was in the
district or not, and quite regardless of whether or not he had children to
go to the school. It was a social gathering, just as barn raisings used to be
in older countries, in Eastern Canada and the United States. The ladies
provided the necessary couple of meals, and small boys were busy water
carriers." The small boys were among the potential twelve children
required by the provincial Department of Education before the permit to
build had been granted.

The secretary-treasurer recorded details of the event for posterity —
the logs that had been cut and hauled from the hills during the previous
winter, already trimmed; the sum paid to the professional carpenter who
had been hired to make doors and windows and to shingle the roof.

"The actual building differed from our farm-house. The wood was
dry, for one thing, so the corners were all dove-tailed and neatly
trimmed. Careful dove-tailing prevented the logs from slipping, each
layer binding the layer immediately below. As the logs were quite long,
holes were bored at intervals, and hardwood dowels used to peg them
together. The carpenter, with a handy assistant, made the doors and
window sashes and fitted them into place as the logs were raised. It was
comparatively easy work until the walls were several feet high. Then it
was necessary to use skids to raise the last few layers."

Few among the builders realized that the architecture chosen had long been used by French and later English pioneers on St. Lawrence River farms and throughout the West as the fur trader-explorers pushed trading posts toward the Pacific. The method had been introduced from Normandy with roof pitches adapted to the heavier Canadian snowfall. Eskdale schoolhouse was a sturdy, warm structure, built to stand for many years beyond most others on the prairie.

Only one serious accident marred the momentous day. As the last timber was being eased up the sloping skids it slipped, felling the man immediately below who was chinking logs already in place. He was badly winded and his back so seriously injured that he was unable to work for the balance of the year. Yet, though the accident put a damper on the festive day, it was not allowed to seriously delay the project. By the time the twin privies at the rear of the school were completed, the weary volunteers had arranged to meet later to install the children's desk-seats and the blackboard, and to put up the heater and stove pipes.

In the meantime the women had prepared supper in the shade of the nearby poplar bluff and father had made a second copper wash boiler of tea. They talked about how to find a teacher and more about plans to help their injured neighbor, resting as well as possible on the floor of his wagon; to do his late haying and to take in his crop, and to help his wife with the chores. When the autumn came, they would also see that his ploughing was not neglected. Inevitably, the cooperative movement in Saskatchewan was on its way.

On the whole, it had been a pleasant day for mother, but the heat had bothered her and she was bone tired from looking after three children excited by the unaccustomed crowds; her arms ached from holding the ten-month-old baby. Otherwise, she would have avoided her sharp retort to father's enthusiastic comment on the professional building achievement. As they jogged homeward in the gathering dusk, he said he wished our house had been as well built because then "it would last forever!"

"Surely, you don't want us to live here forever!" she protested, and then, unable to suppress thoughts that had worried her subconsciously all through the day, she blurted out her hitherto unspoken fears that the school would be too far away for us to attend until we were too old for it. Why had he not insisted on a location nearer his own children's home?

He also was tired, and hurt by her implied criticism of the project on which he had spent so much time and thought and energy.

"You didn't expect me to demand special favors because I am the secretary-treasurer! This is a democratic country!" he reminded her stiffly. Besides, the school was actually less than four miles away. That was no unreasonable walk for country children. In a couple of years or so there would be other children to go along with us; he would buy a driving horse and a buggy and we could take ourselves and them.

Mother was not convinced. The distance was so little under the four miles as to make no difference. We were not old enough to walk there and back every day, and alone. By the time we were old enough — and he could afford that horse and buggy — it would be too late. And what about the winter? What about all the bad weather?

They talked about it all the way home, until with the farmyard in sight, father made his typically optimistic prediction: she must not worry about it. Something would turn up. They would manage all right.

Again, if I am able to understand something of what that momentous summer meant to my mother, I have to rely on my closeness to her. And, of course, on father's recollections.

It was one of those periods in a marriage when each of them was overwhelmed with the pressure of activities on which the welfare and happiness of the other depended. If, while she looked after their children, the house, and the garden, she had managed to listen to all he said, she would have been inordinately proud of him and would more clearly have understood his wonderful dreams of the summer's coming achievements. Actually and inevitably, she had little time for listening. She heard only fragments of what he said.

He had talked so much and so eloquently about the flax, a field he had seeded earlier in June, "on a newly ploughed, lightly cultivated field, quite contrary to Old World methods."

A generous, steady rain followed that seeding and in eight days there was a fine showing of flax: "Almost every seed must have germinated. Yet, in spite of the fine showing I could not accept the theory that freshly ploughed soil should be seeded so lightly."

But a few weeks later the field provided one of the greatest joys of his entire farming experience, the wind-stirred loveliness of a field of flax in bloom, "probably the most beautiful reward that comes to a farmer in the fields of any country." Rarely did farmers pause to look at or study an individual blossom in the development of cereals, most of the flowers of grain being relatively uninteresting as such.

"With flax it is different. Even the passing traveller must see and revel in the sheer beauty of a field of flax in bloom in the morning light, the latest tiny buds unfurled. The blue is like nothing more than the blue of an Italian sky, soft and yet brilliant, intense and yet subdued as it is rippled by the faintest breeze. A field of flax is not easily forgotten."

The flax satisfied some inherited need for visual satisfaction in farming that he would not lightly relinquish, much like the satisfaction he derived from his firm belief in crop rotation.

"By sowing a variety of crops, sufficient time is allowed for seeding and later harvesting, with a minimum of confusion and rush — something very distasteful to an Englishman. Less labor is required this way, and that which is employed is employed for the entire season. We found, too, that with the multi-grain method of farming, there was time to inspect machinery and get each ready for the next crop." He credited his philosophy of farming to "those ancestors whose love of the soil I had inherited." It all led directly to his interest in the Grain Growers movement and the economic problems of marketing.

He had spent hours with W. R. Motherwell, who had been the first president of the Grain Growers Association at its incorporation in 1902. The minister of agriculture, himself a working farmer, shared every settler's need for improved track loading facilities and more railway cars to transport their crops to existing eastern markets and potential west-coast ports, the original and perennial need of prairie grain growers. Like his peers, father also needed a more equitable means of assessing the quality of his grain. Each time he had hauled a load of wheat to the elevator he had resented the necessity of emptying bag after bag into the elevator hopper and accepting valuations that were too often far below standard; more than once meticulously hand-picked grain he knew would warrant No. 1 Hard had been rated No. 2. Either he must accept the iniquitous rating or return home with a load of grain and no cash for everyday living and the purchase of next year's seed. Hauling perfectly dry grain to an elevator and then having it rated moist came close to breaking more than one settler's morale, his own included.

The Ottawa lobbying of some thirty thousand prairie farmers widened father's horizon in 1909. Like most of them, he began to realize that in less than a decade he was no longer completely isolated and entirely on his own resources. Together, less than half a dozen men in his neighborhood had taken part in establishing the Herd Law; less than a score had improved main roads and organized their Local Improvement District. Now, they were uniting to win better market facilities, better prices and were talking about free trade. They had good reason to think of themselves as a potentially strong political force.

Father lacked competent economic advice, and he heartily disliked personal accounting. Had he asked for and accepted mother's advice, they might have avoided some painfully difficult situations. I doubt that it ever occurred to him — and certainly mother would never have suggested such a thing — that the modest sums he spent on good cigars at Fort Qu'Appelle might better be spent on the farm, or on his family. Seldom did he add up the entire costs of his farming operations.

He chose to ignore circumstances that cut into operating costs and an eventual healthy profit: market prices; mice and gophers that devastated harvest stooks; costs of hauling grain to the elevator and occasional hired help. When a crop yielded handsomely he did not want to lessen his satisfaction in it with thoughts of bookkeeping. Nor did he ever quite realize during his actual farming years how enormous an emotional price he and his wife paid for the reality and the dream. Given enough years, he expected to achieve his fondest ambitions, counting on the government eventually to ensure against prolonged low prices such as the sixty-five cents a bushel he had been offered for last summer's No. 1 Hard wheat.

Yet there were times when his judgment about crop prices and the grain markets was unassailable, and he might have been mistaken for a shrewd, practical economist.

We had an abundance of good plain food. When butter sold for twelve cents a pound at the Fort our growing family consumed all that mother churned, and if there was a surplus father used it for axle grease. Bacon at eight cents a pound — as well cured and flavored as any he had seen on an English breakfast table — provided nourishing food and varied the morning porridge. Most years, the garden yielded an ample harvest of roots. We had plenty of milk and eggs.

Through July and into August mother had few qualms about the health and happiness of us, her children. From breakfast time until supper we played out of doors, our days enriched by special moments when she or father, briefly at home during daylight hours, introduced us to various as-yet-unknown occurrences in nature. That was how we learned about the prairie chickens, and how we came to recognize their strange drumming sound. That day we watched Mr. Prairie Chicken dancing with Miss Prairie Chicken, as father described them, he with his head down, wings outstretched, beating the ground with his furry feet; an eager lover trying to attract a mate who was taking her time to make up her mind about accepting him. Father thought they would get married and live happily ever after — just like him and mother.

He showed us the gawky bittern standing on one long leg, feeding beside a slough; when he shot one and it belched up a lizard on the kitchen table, he and mother decided that a bittern would never replace a duck or a prairie chicken as food. It was almost as undesirable as that other *bête noir* of the inexperienced settler, the hell diver whose name we were not allowed to use in any other connection, though father often said it when he discussed Dante's *Inferno* with Mr. Locktie.

We loved the loon and his funny, haunting cry and often watched him dive, trying to guess where he would surface again and how long he would remain underwater. We recognized the handsome grebe duck because father had shot one and carefully skinned and tanned its lovely silvery breast to trim a hat for mother; at the time grebe were fashionable and expensive in London. We learned to avoid skunks after he tanned two fine skins and sent them to England for his sister to wear; according to her letters, every time it rained her beautiful black and white fur scarf literally stank — and in England it rained every day!

Much as snakes terrified mother, a dread I have always shared, he insisted that they were an important link in nature's scheme: "Because they like the mice that every year took an enormous toll of garden produce and grain, snakes are our friends." So were beaver and muskrats, and he caught and tanned scores of muskrats to make insoles for our moccasins. We watched Queenie, our dog, hunt hundreds of gophers in the fields, and badgers throw up mounds of earth around every new hole. We were so accustomed to the night-time howl of coyotes that we seldom consciously heard them. One unforgettable day, I saw three antelope, so near that I could almost have touched them.

At nearly eight years old, I was permitted to go for the mail that the rural mailman left in the box near the Touchwood Trail. Proud of my new responsibility, I had almost reached the box nailed to a well-anchored post when the antelope danced out of a poplar bluff. They were no more than average height, but to a child they looked enormous. Forgetting my errand, I turned and ran. Though mother was sympathetic, father assured me that no wild animal would hurt me if I did not first hurt it. He made me go back and waited until I returned clutching the letters and the newspaper. He then told me that I was a good girl; words from him meant as much to me as they would have done to mother, particularly when he said that he was proud of me.

We spent hours looking for birds' nests, in the poplar trees and bushes, in the grass, or beside a slough. We learned never, never to disturb a nest, and mother knew the names of most of the birds close to the farmyard, and of course, the bird songs. She knew most of the wild flowers, too, and that summer encouraged us to look for clumps of golden lady's slippers and tiger lilies; earlier in the spring she made a game of who spotted the first furry crocus or one of the fragrant, shy violets.

That year, during July and early August everything grew well. They dug the early potatoes and carrots and cooked the tiny beets from thinning along with the tops for a specially delicious meal. The raspberry canes yielded several baskets of rich, plump berries. We had lettuce and green onions, green peas and beans and spinach. The rest of the vegetables promised as fine a harvest as the flax and the oats and barley. Finest of all was the field of new Red Fife wheat on which father had placed his highest hopes since he had ploughed his first furrow.

It was such a splendid field, large by comparison with Yorkshire fields; not a weed could be seen. On the twelfth of August it was already turning a rich golden tan with the promise of forty bushels to the acre. As he gazed across the largest field of wheat he had ever sown, its surface wind-stirred "like the waves of a gentle ocean," father thought it was even more beautiful than the flax.

But there was something strange about the weather that twelfth of August. In spite of the sun's early morning warmth a shiver ran through him as he stood on the knoll in front of the house. Later, as night fell, the full moon was so bright it outshone the stars. The entire atmosphere seemed supernatural.

"During the night the thermometer dropped to five degrees of freezing

— with our wheat in the dough stage. Tragedy stalked through that deceptive, beautiful night, ruining the hopes of a pioneer farmer."

The frost that caught the wheat in the early dough stage shrivelled every kernel in every ear. There would be no substance to be made into fine flour. The bulk was reduced from the anticipated thirty-five or forty bushels to the acre to five or ten, its value to less than thirty cents a bushel.

"Doing a little very simple arithmetic, thirty-five bushels at seventy cents would be $24.50; thirty-five bushels of frozen grain at thirty cents would be $10.50 — and the cost of every operation from seeding to threshing would be as much to the acre."

For father and mother shivering in the early dawn light as they surveyed the ruination of their hopes, their only consolation was the fine fields of oats and barley, father's further vindication of his belief in mixed farming.

The frost had ruined most of the garden. Beets, mangolds, and other soft roots were killed, as were the peas and beans, cauliflower, and cabbages. All that remained to cheer father — mother had lost hope much earlier — was that the late potatoes would grow new leaves and mature as usual. Mother had also lost the lovely buoyant look of health of the earlier summer days when she had almost forgotten our urgent need for schooling; the suntan had faded from her cheeks. The joyous, happy hours ended when she stood beside father and looked across the frozen wheat field where every head that had stood so proudly on its stalk now drooped hopelessly.

For four days mother struggled against her mood of numb grief for herself and her husband and for us children. She was terrified that she might go mad, the fate she dreaded as much for him as for herself. On the fourth day she could bear it no longer. It was the sixteenth of August and my eighth birthday. She waited until father came in to his noon-time dinner, and until we had all finished our meal and she had put the two younger children to bed for their afternoon sleep. Father sat at the table, his chair pushed comfortably back, quietly smoking his pipe, for a moment forgetting the recent calamity.

He had noticed her unusual expression. Her heightened color vaguely reminded him of the pretty, spirited girl whose determination had sent him off to Africa. This time, he could not have sailed away if he had wanted to.

Mother sat in the opposite chair, both hands gripping the edge of the table. Instinct or the strength of her conviction drove her straight to the point. She reminded him of his beloved London college; of the evening when they had hung the parchment recording his admission to the freedom of the City of London, and of the Lord Mayor's dinner at the ancient Guild Hall; the theaters they had loved; his London greenhouse and the darkroom where he had developed so many of his photos. Had he forgotten it all?

Shocked as much by her vehemence as by the reminders of that life that seemed so remote that he might have read about it, he carefully put down his pipe. But she held his eyes as he looked up.

Of course not, he retorted. He had been occupied with the struggle to survive. He had been making a new life, as she very well knew.

All that she acknowledged. He had worked harder than he had ever worked, as she had. But there had been so much to do. After six summers all they could foresee for years to come was more drudgery. Was that all their children could expect?

He began to enumerate their achievements: the house and stable; the fields; the horses and democrat; their place in the community; Eskdale School. The farm would soon begin to show a profit, and they could buy the horse to drive us to school. Soon, we older girls would be able to walk three and a half miles.

That meant seven miles every day, she reminded him, and he countered with his often-repeated assurance that something would happen. In another few years, she would not know Western Canada, the way it was being settled.

But a few years would be too long. Much too long. They would be too old to go to school. They must learn the elements of an education now. It was not enough that they had lessons at home, or that they were happy in their healthy outdoor life. They had refused to eat the oranges he had bought, because they had never seen an orange since coming to Canada. The babies had never seen either an orange or an apple — and even they would be grown up before they did if their parents waited for something to happen. They seldom played with other children. They knew none of the amenities he and she had taken for granted at home.

The usual twenty-minute after-dinner break stretched into an hour of passionate argument on mother's part, efforts to placate her on father's. Nora and I sat very still and quiet, as we had learned to do in such moments of domestic drama, this time concerning us and plans in which we had no voice.

They talked about the boarding school for Indian children at Lebret near Fort Qu'Appelle, but that was too far away. We might be sent to our grandparents in England, but without the wheat crop the farm could not afford such expense, and father insisted that as Canadians we must receive our education in Canada.

In our childish minds we knew how desperately he longed to get back to readying his binder for the oats and barley crop; that only mother's deep concern for our schooling kept him indoors on a mid-August afternoon. We also sensed that to him her preoccupation was a kind of stubbornness with which he was quite familiar, a woman's stubbornness, rare and he might have conceded, very close to courage. But despite his awareness of her anxiety, he shared few of her qualms. Nora and I could read and write, and add and subtract and multiply sums. We knew the songs mother had taught us and the stories he had read to us. Some day, he rather vaguely hoped, we might accomplish what few women actually expected to accomplish — we might find some sort of lucrative careers that could support us, careers suitable for women.

Though he slept well that night, mother did not. For hours she lay awake beside him, careful not to move lest she disturb the sleep he needed. In the morning she still could not forget the thoughts that swirled endlessly in her mind, the conviction that she must do something, that it was not enough merely to hope that something would happen.

For there were anxieties she felt she could not entirely share with him. More than once she had seen the hired man, that nice son of their neighbor, leaving his work to show Nora and me a flower or a bird. She had seen him crawling through the grass with us as we stalked a bluebird's nest; talking to us when he might have been doing something else. It was not that she wanted him to work all the time, nor that she begrudged him or us our fun. It was more than that. With so few other children to play with we naturally looked to him when we wanted a game. We would do so increasingly as we grew up, and it was not a situation she was going to encourage.

She had tried to tell herself that there was nothing bad about it. Nothing naughty. Often she had wanted to discuss it with father, but she could imagine his amused retort. We were just children. We were much too young to get into that sort of trouble. Besides — and she could picture his tolerant smile — every creature sooner or later had to learn about the butterflies and the bees; what could be more natural than observing nature through nature?

For a woman who got about little beyond her own small world, she knew an amazing amount about happenings in the community, often fleshing out the news father shared with her over their late suppers. In no other way could she have heard about the settlers who had abandoned their farm because the municipal school was too remote for their children, and had moved to Kelliher where the husband had already established a small business. While she would not suggest that father do likewise, the move might help her to solve her anxiety and she had no hesitation in suggesting that he approach the couple on his next visit to the village.

I heard about it only several days later when father came home with the momentous news that I was to go to Kelliher to stay with those former neighbors, that he would drive me the thirteen miles early Monday morning and bring me home Friday afternoon. I was going to school.

Nothing had prepared me for going to school. I had never played with other children who had been to school for that frightening first day. It was the last thing I wanted to do. I hated all mother's admonitions that I must be a good girl; sit properly with my knees together like a young lady and not in the hoydenish tomboyish way Nora and I straddled the leopard's stuffed head; never let anyone kiss me on the mouth and remember that nice little girls kissed people on the cheek.

It would all have been an agonizing experience, those weeks when I was being prepared for school, except for the frocks mother made — much nicer than those I wore every day. She made a warm coat from one of her own, Eaton's fabulous catalogue not yet bringing us its tempting array of coatings. Gradually, the fear turned to pride that I was old enough to go to school. Only that panic in the pit of my stomach about leaving home spoiled the excitement that gradually and then swiftly filled me every day.

When the moment came to climb up beside father to the high democrat seat I felt such an awful lump in my throat as well as in my stomach that I could hardly look at mother standing there with Dodie in her arms and Nora and Sybbie silently pressing against her skirt.

The former neighbors I was to stay with were delightful people who lived in a frame house so new that scattered lumber and shingles covered the yard. We had macaroni and cheese for supper the first evening, in a silver casserole, something we had never had at home. It was smooth and creamy and delicious.

During the first recess I stood tongue-tied and shy, watching a big boy of fourteen showing the other little girls who were at school for the first time the right way to pee. My hostess's daughter, who was my own age, and a couple of others of wider experience scornfully told him that they knew all about it and to my own surprise, I wanted to tell him that little girls did not pee, they wee-weed. But I said nothing. Something, as well as my shyness, had warned me not to talk to people about that sort of thing, in the same way that I already knew there were other things I must not tell my hosts.

Just before the school bell rang the crestfallen show-off told the grade-one listeners how fathers climbed on top of mothers in bed to make babies — just like the bull and the stallion behind the barn. While at the time I knew my father would never do such a bad thing, I eventually learned that boasting had to be part of going to a new frontier school; that until lessons added fresh dimensions, children who lived on isolated farms naturally talked of things they had experienced or heard about in the family. They were merely trying to overcome their first awareness of loneliness and longing for home.

But the major lessons I learned during my first days at school were to be quiet and to sit for a long time on a hard seat, both irksome and seemingly unfair. Before I could learn anything more exciting, one morning my hostess looked very hard at my hair as she brushed it. The next morning she looked at it even more closely, and again brushed it very hard. To my surprise, when father came to get me on Friday afternoon, she had all my clothes packed ready to go home. I was not coming back again on Monday morning as I had expected.

Those kind people had sent a telegram to father at LeRoss; the first phone line had not yet been strung between the villages. Only when I was home again and he had talked to mother did I learn the shocking reason for being sent home. I had nits in my hair.

I had not been naughty. I had tried to be a good girl, but the news upset mother as much as if I had done all the things she had told me not to do. She was naturally embarrassed, as I realized from what she said when she looked at my hair as the lady in Kelliher had done and parted it carefully. She washed it with strong soap and rubbed my head very hard with smelly coal oil. She did it again next day, though she usually washed my hair only once every week.

Sometimes there were tears in her eyes, and she rubbed so hard that her fingers hurt my scalp. In a way, it felt as though she was blaming me for getting those lice in my hair, though I had not known they were there. She said that though she was terribly embarrassed, that was not the worst thing. The worst thing was that she did not know what to do next. I might never have another opportunity to go to school. Nor Nora nor the babies. When she talked that way, I knew there was something that troubled her more than the fact of my disgrace, something worse than having her eldest child sent home because the other little girl might catch some of those lice in her hair.

She, and I, would have felt much better if we had then heard the news father brought home a couple of weeks later. Every head in the school, he reported, had lice, and the smell of coal oil had sickened the new young teacher from Ontario. But I never returned to Kelliher because yet another calamity, very much worse, further blighted mother's hopes.

Mother was alone with us children when it occurred. Father had gone to LeRoss, and the temporary hired man was away helping his own father with his stooking.

She was kneading a squeaky batch of bread dough into loaves, and when she set them to rise on the back of the stove she realized that the sky had darkened ominously. Hoping that father would get home before the rain started, she gave us our dinner. By that time it was so dark that she thought about lighting a lamp. Her hand about to lift the glass chimney, she decided not to; she had never lit a lamp in the middle of the day and the storm would likely soon blow over.

The wind was so strong that she ran out to shut the stable door and to check the catch on the ice house. She closed every window in the house and as she slammed the back door a great gust almost knocked her off her feet. Terrified, she realized that she could hardly see the stable. The wind-blown rain had obliterated her view of the nearest corner of the field of oats.

The tone of her voice, halfway between a scream and a groan, frightened me. I had never before heard her say "Oh God!" like that. I knew she was terrified because she actually consulted me. What could she do if it was a cyclone, if it ripped off the roof, if lightning struck a tree and caused a fire? And, where was father?

Though she had just put Sybbie and Dodie in bed for their afternoon nap, she wakened them and, with the baby in her arms and us others huddled together beside her, she stood by the north window, peering out for the first glimpse of him.

Hail stones as large as pigeon eggs hammered at the window. Smaller stones whitened the ground near the house like snow. Anxious that she, too, might whimper as we were whimpering, she turned and went to the stove. She looked at the loaves under the tea cloth and hesitated to lift the lid to put another stick of wood on the fire. But we needed the bread. As she checked the damper the awful sound of the wind howled down the chimney, loud above its lashing against the log walls and the shrieking under the eaves.

The storm passed as quickly as it had struck. In minutes the charged air cleared. She could see the stable again. She could see the field of oats, as flat as though a steam roller had passed over it, the field on which father had invested his hopes ever since frost had killed the wheat.

Her first shocked thoughts were for him. He had counted so much on the oats. He had never believed that such a catastrophe could occur, that the oats as well as the wheat could be ruined. She had to force herself to wait long enough to take the precious golden loaves from the oven before she wrapped a shawl about Dodie and, with the rest of us traipsing beside her, trudged through the melting hail stones and the wet grass toward the field. Before she reached it, father drove into the yard at a crawl that reminded her of the oxen, his anguish eloquent in the droop of his shoulders and head. Like a tired, old man he got down from the rig.

They had no words for one another. Nothing they could say could alter their mutual loss. The field that yesterday had been such a glorious sight, today mocked their every hope. Every heavy stalk that had been rich with ripened kernels of grain lay as flat as though it had been carefully placed by giant taunting hands.

Mother stood mute, the center of our tiny group, the baby still in her arms. Together we watched father walk slowly around the entire perimeter of the field, up and down and across. We saw him bend and break off one of the stalks as again he circled the field. Mother feared that he might be going mad, and was terrified for her own sanity.

That day he faced the chilling prospect of failure and somehow replaced it with a determination to persevere. As though he did not realize what he was doing, he took the heavy child from his wife's arms and brusquely commanded her to "come with me!" Together the rest of us trudged behind his every quickening step, up and across and down the width and length of the field.

The near cyclonic wind that accompanied the hail had beaten out a heavy toll of kernels and damaged some of the straw. But the loss was by no means total. With careful cutting, he estimated that he could salvage most of it.

He unhitched the patient horses, standing where he had left them as he joined mother at the field, and carried feed and water. Then he sat down in the living room to plan some means of reclaiming the crop. Because it had been ready to harvest he had repaired and oiled the binder and next day, when the field had dried under a hot sun, he rode out of the yard, silent on the seat of the machine.

The oats lay mainly from south to north, so he cut a swath against the lay of the grain. Even with four horses and a six-foot binder it was so heavy that it clogged the machine. When he cleared the binder and cut a narrower swath, the sheaves tumbled out in a wonderfully heartening stream. Patiently, hour after hour he continued to cut each narrow row as the binder lifted the heavy grain. With every swath the burden of anxiety he had not shared with mother gradually eased; he had not reminded her, if she had ever really known of the awful fact, that whether the crop was a complete failure or not, he must pay the heavy threshing bill for which he had contracted.

"I was so confident that the crop would still give us a big yield that I felt the time required to harvest it would be repaid," he told her later. "And it did! Some of the grain had been damaged, it is true, but after harvesting we had over three thousand bushels of very fine oats, at the rate of eighty-two bushels to the acre."

His splendid hopes received a severe jolt when he hauled his first load of the oats to the grain elevator. Whether because the year had been especially good for oats or because the grain dealers faced a glut, the price he was offered fell short of what he felt it was worth. Unwilling to haul the load home, he arranged with the elevator manager to store it until spring, hoping it would bring a much higher price when he offered it for seed.

In a decision that was part gallantry, part bruised pride, he did not tell mother that after he had paid the threshers' bill, very little capital remained to see us through the winter; she would never understand that farmers south of the valley, and in much more settled country, paid the threshers between six and eight cents a bushel for oats and barley and that the price was naturally higher for farmers living thirty miles farther north.

There were times, and that was one of them, when briefly he remembered the ancient Roman threshing floor he had seen when he and Jos crossed France on their return from Africa. Flailing his first few bushels of grain by hand, or using the oxen to tramp out the kernels on the ice on a slough, had been a step he never wanted to recall, but he could not forget either primitive method in the first hurt of his own disappointment.

Mother's disappointment was even greater. She lacked his sanguine belief in the market and, not daring to count on the cash he expected in the spring, she had to forego the comfortable satisfaction of planning new clothes for us children or necessities for the household. She worried about how we could get through the next six or eight months. She could not share his belief in the future value of the barley crop either, the fourteen hundred bushels of the finest barley he had ever seen that had met with the same disappointing valuation as the oats. It, too, he decided to store for the winter. At twenty cents a bushel he felt he had no choice but to shoulder this further financial burden.

For her there seemed to be no ray of hope; assurances of the payments that would come in the spring could not console her for the fact that without the bountiful vegetable crop they had counted on before the frost ruined it, they had to buy potatoes before the winter was over. They were back where they had been during those first spare years, dependent on wild game and the steer for beef — that and father's small income from his municipal duties and as a justice of the peace.

There were days when she forgot about the gramophone, and he did not remind her.

They had sympathized feelingly with a settler whose second-year wheat field had been ruined by the frost. When the cyclone flattened the unfortunate man's oats and barley, father had offered to retrieve some of the loss as he had done with his own. But there was nothing to cut. The oats lay in flat windrows of stalks with empty heads, the kernels flailed into the ground where the only hope was that they would germinate next spring. That had not been enough for the settler's pregnant wife.

For several weeks she grieved over their desperate situation and early on the morning after the first autumn frost, her husband called on father as the local justice of the peace. During the night his wife had waded through the thin ice to the deepest part of the nearest large slough. In a completely emotionless voice he said he had come to report the suicide.

It was the first in the community, and one of the most heartbreaking of father's several terms as local magistrate.

Mother could not rid herself of the burden of the young woman's appalling unhappiness that had driven her to take not only her own life but also that of the child she carried, nor could she forget the aching loneliness of the bereaved husband and his agonized feeling of responsibility no matter how splendid his intentions had been. She shuddered to think of that bitterly cold, slimey slough and of the strange courage that had driven the woman so far into it.

When father returned from the simple funeral — lacking the consolation of a clergyman's more formal commital service he had read the twenty-third psalm as he once had done following a death in Africa — he found mother so distraught that she frightened him.

After supper she sat on Nora's bed and answered some of our questions about death, but not many. She said she could not sing to us either; tomorrow evening she would sing whatever we liked. For long silent moments she looked at the *Kyrie*, still luminous against a star-lit sky. She seemed to be looking at it and yet not really seeing the choristers until father spoke to her from the doorway. Without taking her eyes from the picture she said, as much to herself as to him or to us, "Lord have mercy on us." She said the words as though they were a prayer. Then a little self-consciously, she kissed us both and turned down the lamp on its bracket.

Father kissed us and lowered the cretonne curtain, but not before we saw him put his arm around her waist. A few minutes later, we heard him wind the gramophone and play the *Tannhäuser* aria, "The Evening Star."

Mother was still very quiet in the morning, but it was a different quietness. Her eyes were still very large and dark with that lovely, secret smile that reassured us all. By some strange sense I knew then that she would never wade into a slough.

The Diary

It was late November, the days so short that they had to light the lamp for breakfast and supper, the evenings so long that when father was away she often managed with candles to conserve the precious coal oil. Their worst November, it seemed, because her hopes were as dark as the longest, dreary, lonely evening.

By half past seven she had tucked the little ones into bed. She had sung the "Away in a Manger" she was teaching Nora and me, and she had mentally measured the space at the foot of the cot against the wall to see if there was room for another because Sybbie at three was already too big for the crib in their bedroom. She knew, as she had known for weeks, that the only solution was for us to double up, and she wondered which way would be the most harmonious or cause the least trouble.

The house was so quiet that the sharp crack of a log in the stove made her jump, her ears straining for the sound of the sleigh bells she could not expect for at least an hour, possibly two or three. To take her mind off the turmoil of her apprehensions she stood for a moment beside the kitchen stove, listening to the comforting hum of the kettle, before clearing our supper dishes from the table. Then she laid places for herself and father, chores that took only minutes. Tonight she could not settle to her mending or heat the irons for the pinafores and aprons and the table cloth she had washed earlier in the day. When she realized that she was pacing faster and faster up and down the room, she made herself stop, look out the frost-patterned windows, pick up a plaything from the floor, straighten a knife and fork on the table — anything to discipline the agitation that frightened her.

How long could they go on like this, six people living on that tiny salary from the municipality? No vegetables except the couple of bags of potatoes that already had dwindled alarmingly and the cabbages and carrots and turnips father had bought from a neighbor who had escaped the frost? The steer he had killed and stored on the roof might last until the end of January, but not much longer. The new cow was not due to calve until March, and they might be short of milk. The crocks of butter in the cellar and the eggs in the brine would not last all winter, either. And that was not all she had to worry about.

Though she had made games of lessons, morning after morning, she could not think up games to keep us older children occupied for ever, nor expect to teach four children around the table. Even with the songs we were learning, the fun we enjoyed as we warbled together, she felt she could not much longer endure the months and years crowded into the one small sitting room. Nor the isolation. The possibility of yet another child.

No. Not that. Not another child. She dared not let herself think about that most likely possibility. For a moment the thought of it forced her into the rocking chair. But it was not long before she got up and again paced the floor, pausing in front of the gramophone. For a moment the tensions eased. She had never trusted herself to wind the handle and place a record on the little spindle, yet, as always since the evening when father had brought it home, she felt a surge of emotion that was close to rapture. She would not touch it alone even now, but it was there. That was as much a source of consolation as the fact that father had thought about and bought it.

The thought made her briefly happy. She turned and looked up at the framed parchment bearing the signature of the Lord Mayor of London; at the little shelf of books and then at the diary.

She had not looked at the diary for years, not really to see it, to think about its significance. Now she reached up and took it in her hands, blew off the dust that had settled on top between the hard covers, opened the front page, and read the neat inscription "To my dearest Nellie" and the date of the first entry: September 1896, South Africa.

Her thumb marking the significant first page, she went back to the rocking chair, closer to the candles, and began to read the closely written neat lines that had been his first record of his reaction to her refusal to accompany him.

That page, and the next and the next, she had read with delight, forgetting why she had sent him away. Tonight she read with the wry awareness that she would have made the same refusal, even on second thought and with the full, disturbing knowledge that she loved him as she could never love another man. In the quiet, lonely farmhouse, longing for something happy to think about, she did not want to read on, to feel again the aversion she had felt for the harsh, primitive life he so obviously enjoyed. She hated this life as much as she would have hated pioneering in Africa; that she had to admit to be honest with herself. But she had married her Will. They had shared more than nine years of intimacy and some disagreement, years that could not be undone.

Sitting, quiet now, in the rocking chair, she knew that she did not want to undo those years. She merely wished that they had been different, that the years to come would be different. The kettle boiled on, another stick of wood fell in the stove, and she did not read further into the closely written accounts of stalking and killing lions, narrow escapes from thundering water buffalo, or malaria in a fever hell in a Portuguese East African hospital. It would take every effort of self discipline she could muster to continue to live with the present life, but she knew she would do it somehow, as long as she lived. She would rather live with the man she loved under the circumstances she knew — and disliked to the point of hatred on many an occasion — than live without him. The fact of the diary had proved, if she had ever doubted, that he loved her. He had taken the course that he felt would be best for her and for their children. In a way it, the diary, was like another marriage contract. She had accepted it for better or for worse.

Yet along with her moments of premonition or presentiment, or perhaps because of them, she was a clear-thinking woman. The facts she had faced during those long minutes in the rocking chair did not blind her to the facts that disturbed her. She had merely become more sharply aware of her responsibilities to her children, the children that dear man had fathered. No problem loomed larger or more commandingly than the need to find some enlightening future for them.

Again, she got up and walked the length of the room, but she no longer paced so fast that she frightened herself. Pausing at the south window, she shook off the shiver that caught her briefly, and looked long at the cold, moonlit snow that blanketed everything — the naked poplar bluff, the pump handle pointing like an upraised arm, the shadow of the ice house. When she turned to look out the north window she saw the stable muffled under its snow-blanketed roof and beside it, above the drifts piled against its still unpainted walls, the tiny W.C. The teepee of uncut firewood looked like a new, white bell tent. Beyond the stable the hay stacks were white bee hives flanking the new granary that held the oats and barley, cleaned and bagged ready for spring seeding.

That was her world. Her little, lonely, isolated world that belonged to her husband and their children. The world so unlike the world he had so often described when he was dreaming his dreams and making his plans for the new-world farm where he would proudly extend the fabulous British Empire in which she believed as fanatically as he did.

The snow tonight was so cold and beautiful that it, too, frightened her. There was something in its moonlit clarity that showed up details that the sun had never shown her. Not another sign of human habitation dared to challenge its supremacy, not another flickering stable lamp or a glimmer from a settler's kitchen.

Trying to imagine that night when I was there with her, a sleeping child, I have gradually come to understand something of her feeling since, late in the twentieth century, in a brightly lit study in a brightly lit city, I read D. G. Jones' lines from "Kate, These Flowers . . ."

> Loneliness becomes us, we
> advance through separations, learning
> to love cold skies, empty
> even in the last high
> hail and farewell of birds
> arrowing south
>   wilderness
> waste fields become us[1]

That was what she knew, though she had no reference in her experience to describe her feelings. It was what she dreaded deep in her being, more than she anguished over the lack of adequate schooling for us, her children: the threat of succumbing to those waste fields of loneliness that were a fact of every settler's life.

With something of the awful clarity with which the moon lit the wind-sculpted snow, she sensed the possible effects of isolation and enforced solitude. In the sparsely settled Canadian Northwest it was as real as every rich potential and as menacing as hail and frost and the prairie fire she would never forget. It could turn men and women, and particularly women who lived most of their days and years alone with their young children, in on themselves, numbly content with nothing beyond their own dwindling resources. It could mean the end of dreams and the denial of vision.

She had commenced to pace the floor again, in spite of her determination not to. The north window was almost clear of its frost patterns, so often had she rubbed the glass as she peered into the night, wondering if she had failed to hear the jingle of the sleigh bells. When at last she heard them clearly — she had known for a couple of hours that she could never miss that sound — it was nearly ten o'clock. He was not often as late when he had been to LeRoss for his weekly meeting.

She was at the door before he opened it, eager for the sound of his voice, for his reassurances that nothing serious had happened to delay him; he had merely called in at John George's farm and found the reeve and his family about to sit down to their supper and had accepted Mrs. George's invitation to join them.

As he reached for the stable lamp and lit it, he noticed the two places still untouched at their own table. Contrite, he scolded her for waiting so long and told her she must never do it again. Promising to share all the news as soon as he finished his evening chores, he slammed the door against the cold.

It was so like him, she reflected, not to realize that she could not eat her own meal when she had no knowledge of when he would return. He

1. Reprinted with permission of General Publishing Co. Limited from *A Throw of Particles: The New and Selected Poetry of D. G. Jones* (Toronto, 1983).

knew nothing about solitude and loneliness. She need have no concern that he would succumb to the very real effects of isolation, as she and the children might. When she had put away his knife and fork — she left a spoon for the hot soup he liked after a long, cold drive — she sat down to eat the breast of wild duck she had braised. From her own place at the table she could see the dim, flickering stable light and, watching it, she thought bitterly that she was like the cow he was milking. She could not swallow the food she chewed, her appetite had completely gone.

Was her life, their life, always to be like this? Must she always shape her days and evenings and even her nights to mesh with the uncertain times of his going and his returning? Banish her loneliness and growing dread of too much solitude at the sound of the sleigh bells sharp across the snow? Yet, as suddenly as the testy mood struck her, she remembered his hearty home-coming greeting, his obvious delight as he opened the door, his eagerness to share the news of his day.

Seated opposite him as he supped his soup half an hour later, she scarcely noticed the too-familiar, acrid stable smell that he always brought in on his clothes after milking. She was no longer alone. All those corroding feelings of isolation were forgotten.

He had finished his soup by the time he mentioned the John Deere Plough Company that was going to open a sales branch at LeRoss; that showed what an established eastern firm thought about the future of the West and in particular their own municipality. The company had purchased a lot near Mitchells' new general store and had already ordered lumber for the shed at Gingra's yard. Father had met the representative who was setting up the agency and had been shown the list of implements that would be available by the spring; he had ordered one of the ploughs.

She had been so enthusiastic about the store and hearing about the family who owned it that for a moment she failed to realize the significance of his order for yet another plough.

He had bought a plough only two years ago, a very modern implement to replace the original primitive single share; why did he want to buy another plough now? How could he afford it? How could he pay for it with the summer's wheat a total loss and the oats and barley still in storage?

Father replied with his usual assurance that she need not worry; the money would be available well before the bill arrived.

But would it? she argued. How could he be so sure that the grain would bring a good price? That he could sell it at all?

His happy, assured mood changed as he sensed her hostile reaction and with it, hers. The usual late evening warmth became a chilly gulf between them, and she had the unreasonable feeling that she had caused it. Even worse was the realization that again they had allowed a difference to separate them, a situation she felt she might have prevented had she been less testy in voicing her apprehension. Yet now she could not prevent herself from reminding him that if there was any money to spare, it should be spent on the children's schooling. They needed more books. They needed warm coats before they could go to any school.

It was that August after-dinner hour again, but sharper and with a bitterness neither had experienced. He had no answer to her charges and, contrite, she could say nothing to heal the breach. For the first time in the log house they went to bed hostile and angry.

She hated him when she heard his even, relaxed breathing; he had slept almost as soon as he lay stiffly stretched out on his own side of the bed. For her, the minutes became aching hours as she told herself that her loyalty to him included loyalty to their children's needs, giving them a proper upbringing, showing them that there was a way of living better than this primitive existence that he repeatedly promised would end, but that showed little evidence that it ever would end before they were too old to enjoy it.

She thought about her promise to love and obey him, and she firmly believed that it was part of that duty to do for the children what he could not — or did not — do for them; that her responsibilities as a mother were as binding as those of a wife to her husband.

Lying close beside him, every touch of his body as he turned in his sleep became an agony. She knew then that in all the world there could be no greater, unwanted solitude for two people who loved one another — or who had loved one another — than to share their bed in anger. The anger might have persisted but for his habit of rolling the blankets about him as he turned until she was completely uncovered. As usual when that occurred and his back felt cold, he unrolled the blankets. Tucking them around her, he drew her shivering body close.

She had to respond.

Next morning he seemed to have forgotten their differences. Not so mother. Though she felt happy in their reconciliation, she was more keenly aware than ever of what continued isolation could mean to us. She could do little to change father, of that she had been left with few doubts. But there must be something she could do to prevent, perhaps to overcome, the shyness we had shown on each of the few recent occasions when we met other children and even moreso on meeting strange adults. She understood it because she had found herself hesitating to meet people. We were all becoming ingrown, all except father, and it was something he could not understand.

The new teacher at the new school that was too far away for Nora and me to walk to was a bright, pleasant girl from Ontario. Mother had only met her briefly, but she mustered her determination to relieve our isolation by sending her an invitation to dinner; father could take it on his way to LeRoss. An unexpected aspect of the visit was the teacher's offer to show her, and us, how to make a Christmas tree from a nicely shaped, bare poplar. Before her brother came to drive her home to his house where she boarded, she and mother had ironed every bit of green tissue paper mother could find, cut it into strips, and together we had wound it about the naked limbs. We made gay paper chains from other scraps of colored paper, and everyone had forgotten any shyness they might otherwise have felt.

Much came from that inspired visit. Mother suggested that some of her sheets of music might be useful when the teacher coached her nine pupils for the Christmas concert. She asked father to enquire around the municipality for people who had instruments and would be willing to form a very simple little chamber music group. To her delight a Hungarian settler accepted on condition that he could bring his wife and his two children with him and, of course, his violin; from him, we Wilkins children heard our first lilting Viennese waltzes. The Ukrainian family danced their swift, exciting steps until father warned that the floor beams might be inadequate for any more of them. With the German neighbor and his accordion, and an American bachelor's mouth organ, mother began to discuss repertoires; though they could have no time for rehearsals, they decided to do their best as an addition to the new school's first concert program.

It was a terrible performance, but poignantly gallant and possible only through the universality of music and loneliness. When the pupils, the teacher, and most of the very mixed little audience joined in the songs mother had introduced, the teacher announced some Canadian songs: "The Maple Leaf Forever" and "O Canada" and "Now the Moon Shines Bright on Pretty Redwing," the most popular and familiar of all.

After each pupil had stumbled over recitations culled from the works of well-known Canadian poets and well-known anthologies, the women opened their supper baskets and exchanged cakes and cookies and promising recipes with their neighbors. The only unhappy memory of the evening for us children occurred when the reeve gave each pupil a real Christmas present, a new slate or new pencils or a pencil box; we who did not go to school received none, an omission that troubled mother as much as it did us. When we opened our Christmas stockings a week later, Nora and I each found one of the little pencil boxes with a slide top.

Every present we received that Christmas Day, with the exception of the pencil boxes, indicated how pinched was the state of the Wilkins' finances: the tree had been trimmed by mother and the teacher and us children; she had made the dolls for each of us, with clothes that Nora and I could put on and take off, and cuddly rag dolls for Sylvia and Dorothy. Father had made an embroidery hoop for me, soaking the handle of an old basket in warm water and bending it to form the two matching rings; mother promised to teach me some embroidery stitches.

We had visitors, two Eastern Canadian bachelors, for the roast beef dinner and the English plum pudding. The only items that had cost money were the turnips and carrots and cabbages father had purchased from the farmer who had escaped the killing August frost.

It would have been a completely happy Christmas for us children but for two incidents that not even Nora and I fully appreciated at the time. When he and the guests smoked the cigars one of bachelors had brought, father mentioned the John Deere Company plough that he had ordered; mother, he remarked, teasing her, had not approved the proposed purchase of a larger implement but she would when she saw how much every additional ploughshare increased their production. Remembering the brochure in his pocket, he got up to fetch it, and the three men pored over it while mother cleared the table.

Watching them, her memories went back to the weeks and months in England when every newspaper and broadsheet she had picked up beside father's chair was turned to descriptions of life in Western Canada. Ruefully, she thought that there was no escape for her, there never would be, from this harsh, struggling farm life that fulfilled his every hope and his every dream. Yet, much as she had tried to force herself to understand whatever it was in his nature that craved life on the land, she could not feel that it was right for him to buy that plough until he had actually sold the oats and barley.

The other incident that neither she nor father could completely forget occurred after supper, when we children were in bed.

He had wound the handle on the side of the gramophone and at the first sounds of music Nora and I sat up to listen. Suddenly, mother cried out. Not that, she said, her voice strangely sharp. Anything else, please. Something happier than "The Stars Are Shining," the lament on which, almost, we were nurtured.

At the time father made no protest, and we could not see any special look that may have passed between them. He played every other record in their modest collection — the selections from *H.M.S. Pinafore,* others from *The Bohemian Girl,* and one that came as a surprise to mother — it was the only thing on which he spent any money that Christmas — Nellie Melba singing Schubert's "Ave Maria."

Only many years later, when I began to put together the events of that pioneering decade, did I realize why in her prescience she could not now listen to the *Tosca* aria. Or understand father's unquestioning reaction that must have been as intuitive as hers.

The weather had been much the same every January since they emigrated, bitterly cold, the wind so strong that it whipped up particles of snow sharp enough to cut your cheeks and hurt your eyes. Mother thought it must be like a desert sand storm as she watched father's humped back bent over the sawhorse and the buck saw, the wind blowing every speck of sawdust over the freshly sawn pile of firewood. She wished she could feed fewer sticks into the voracious stove and heater so as to save him some of the daily labor, and when she could bear watching him no longer she turned from the window, steadying herself a moment against the table, longing for some of his physical stamina.

She felt better when he came indoors, stamping his feet, flailing his arms across his chest to speed up the circulation in his numbed hands. His face was ruddy with the look of sturdy good health. He actually had enjoyed sawing wood in that bitter cold, just as he enjoyed carrying water and food to the horses and heaving manure from the stable, and she envied him the enjoyment as much as she hated her own lack of energy and the occasional moments of nausea.

When he went back to his sawhorse, she wanted to dress us children in our outdoor clothes and play the games we enjoyed, racing around the yard as she knew other women did; she always knew more about her neighbors than she realized and that day, because she felt too weary to dress four children and herself, she promised instead to make a batch of crisp ginger cookies like those Mrs. Parker had sent us for Christmas.

For a moment she sat down in the rocking chair, feeling that the brilliant sun and the wind lashing about the house were becoming too stimulating for her. But she knew, as she had known for days, that she could not blame her queasiness on the climate. Like her sudden irritation over the gramophone recording of "The Stars Are Shining" on Christmas Day, and the lassitude, it was all part of a familiar experience. She was again pregnant, worried desperately about where to put yet another cot in the already overcrowded house.

Father, coming in with another armful of firewood, laid it in the box beside the cook stove and turned to look at her. After her four pregnancies, he sensed what had been troubling her. As much to relieve her distress as his own concern, he teased her about the son they both needed and she, sick in heart and body, heard only the teasing and not his affectionate voice. This was no time to talk about a son, she retorted, not without a school within walking distance. Unhappily aware that nothing he could say at the moment would please her, he remained silent. That, too, annoyed her. When he pulled on his mitts to go out again, she tried to suppress her scream.

It was like a kettle boiling over, the sight of him pulling on his mitts, apparently not caring about her condition. She turned on me, accusing me for making so much noise and then, utterly unlike her usual reaction to a noisy child, spanked me with the back of a hair brush. She told me to stop grizzling, and because it had been such a seemingly undeserved punishment, I turned to father.

Like the fabled horseshoe nail that lost the battle, my childish gesture started a storm that frightened us all and eventually contributed to our enormously changed lives.

Mother turned on us both, her voice still unusually sharp. It was father's fault that I had misbehaved. If I had been at school instead of romping around the house this sort of thing would never have happened. A child of eight should be in school. She accused him of forgetting the promise he made last August to do something about schooling if we had a good crop.

Testy and challenged, he retorted that he had not forgotten; he had said we would talk about it when he sold the oats and the barley and that had been a promise he intended to keep. Tying the ear flaps of his cap under his chin, he opened and slammed the door.

Stunned by his reaction and by her own outburst, she stood looking at that closed door, so quiet that we children were also forced into silence. Without being told to we scuttled off to our bedroom, subdued and frightened. Our unusual quiet heightened the sudden crash in the sitting room and her anguished cry. We rushed back into the room where we found her sitting on the floor beside the big picture that had slipped from its hook, its glass shattered. The door that father slammed had probably loosened the hook but so practical and obvious an explanation had not occurred to her. Her arms clasped tightly about her body, she rocked from side to side, her voice no more than a whisper.

Someone is going to die, she moaned. Someone is going to die. Someone always dies when a picture falls. It always happened that way in her family, she reminded herself and us. It always happened. . . . She saw us huddled together and she got up to assure us it was all right and to gather us into her arms. She told me to bring the broom and the dust pan, but instead of sweeping up the broken glass she went into the kitchen to get dinner ready; we were not to wait for father because he was going to saw more wood than usual and pile it beside the door, enough for a couple of days or more.

That was another ominous fact about the day; we were in for a storm, he had said, the big storm of the winter judging by the sun dogs in the western sky, and he had already checked the clothesline strung between the house and the stable so that he could follow it to feed and water the animals if the blizzard cut visibility completely.

I still remembered that day when I watched my husband tap the barometer and say that it was falling fast; mother used to pretend she had not heard father say it because the gesture always gave her the blues.

The sky was darkening when he brought in the last extra armful of firewood and hung up his coat and cap and took off his felt boots. He sat down to his meal with the comfortable assurance of a man who had done everything he could against the storm, at his usual place on the opposite side of the table where he did not notice the shattered picture, still lying where it had fallen. He had not yet noticed the blank space on the wall, nor mother's quiet, withdrawn mood. For him, the farmer's ancient right to his twenty minutes after dinner took precedence over most domestic situations.

Mother had put the little ones to bed for their afternoon rest. As she came back into the sitting room, suddenly she saw the glass on the floor and she lost her quiet, studied composure. Her agonized cry brought father to her in an instant. Scarcely seeing the fallen picture, he carried her to the rocking chair, his arm firm about her shoulders, oblivious of Nora and me standing quiet beside our bedroom doorway, as quiet and frightened as we had been earlier in the morning. Tenderly, he talked to her as he kneeled beside her, brushing her hair gently with his hand.

We had never seen him like this. We had never heard the reassuring voice that told her it was a good thing that Whistler's *Carlyle* and not the *Kyrie* had fallen; the two sheets of glass on the *Kyrie* would have made a much worse mess.

Mention of the *Kyrie* that had become a beloved symbol failed to comfort her. Instead, it roused again the terrible anguish she had associated with the fallen picture. She became hysterical. In a high, terrifying voice she accused him of wanting a new plough more than an education for his children. She said dreadful things about the diary and all his African souvenirs, about Canada and its hardships, about storms and prairie fires — all garbled together. It was as though every thought she had suppressed since he returned from Africa had broken out of the safe in which her love had locked it. Her agonized awareness of what she thought of as disloyalty drove her words like the wind that was mounting its attack on the house.

Nothing father could say or do calmed her. In her present terrible distress she could not calm herself with his assurances that he had done it all for her and the children; that he had chosen a way of life that he knew eventually would be right for us all.

He became almost as distraught as she was. The tragedy of the young English bride, now committed for life to the new mental institution and her child to adoption by strangers, flashed through his mind. He saw again the grotesque body of his neighbor's wife as they pulled her from the slough, swollen with her unborn child. Though he was not a violent man, only one course was obvious to him. He knew he must break her hysterical emotional storm before it became madness. In his desperation he resorted to the treatment that sometimes ended a child's tantrum, a swift sharp spanking. He reached for the sjambok hanging on the wall.

The awful gesture sobered mother. Clutching Nora and me, now suddenly at her side, she swept us into her bedroom with the little ones and shut the door.

How they reconciled that terrifying domestic situation I do not know, but from what I can recreate, I know that they each accepted some of the blame. They admitted that their brief passion would never have occurred under easier circumstances: the diary implicit with as much happiness as pain for mother was as binding on him as on her. While the storm reached its shrieking crescendo and at noon they lighted the bracket lamps, they knew the weather had merely triggered her reaction to the crash of the *Carlyle.* She lacked the physical stamina — and not only when she was pregnant — to continue with either the hard work or to undertake many of the lovely diversions she had dreamed about as her personal means of combatting isolation. Father's attitude toward what hitherto he had regarded as normal feminine psychological changes due to pregnancy changed enormously.

Some time before the storm eased he suggested a compromise: he would build a house in LeRoss where we could go to school, while he himself spent his weekdays on the farm, joining us for the weekends. He would find a man to live on the place, one he could trust to carry out his instructions. They would make do with the smaller revenue and his salary from the municipality. If that was not enough he might look into taking on an agency for that plough company. Somehow he had almost convinced mother that the sale of the oats and barley would make it all possible.

If ever children stood to profit from their parents' behavior, we learned the sublime truth about one fundamental aspect of human relativity: young as we were we could not fail to sense that for people who love one another, there is no greater joy than reconciliation after a bitterly cruel misunderstanding.

For the remainder of that winter father spent much more time than usual in the crowded little house. He kept the wood boxes filled and brought in pails of snow and often melted the snow before he filled the hot water boiler at the back of the cook stove. He carried the flat pans of milk down to the cellar, sharing mother's hope that the cow's milk would last until spring. Sometimes, when he had to leave on municipal affairs, he took Nora and me with him to relieve the house's confusion as much as to divert his mind from the awful threat to his beloved farm life that had begun to haunt him.

As for mother, her spirits improved as she passed the trying early months of pregnancy. At that stage she only partly realized the significance of father's acceptance of her condition. She was so happy in his promise that we should go to school before it was too late to benefit us that again she sang to us at bedtime. Her eyes sparkled and she smiled her former easy smile. She enjoyed the records he played, and talked about others she would like to have. She was a woman who would have become serene and beautiful if she had lived to a great age.

In May we had all marvelled at the sight of Halley's comet through our west bedroom window — father said that watching the comet linked us with the rest of the world — when he drove to LeRoss and returned with the news that mother had not dared to expect: he had sold the oats and the barley.

Impressed by the obvious quality of the oats before hauling them to LeRoss he had weighed a bushel; his belief in his judgment had been vindicated. The 50 ¾ pounds was only a quarter pound less than the oats that had won first prize at the last Regina Agricultural Fair. Sold as seed grain, it easily paid for the winter storage plus a well-merited bonus.

He was as fortunate with the fourteen hundred bushels of barley. At Fort William it graded No. 3, "the highest grade on the Winnipeg Grain Exchange at the time." With the premium father received, the barley yielded thirty-four cents a bushel clear.

His first thought when he realized how splendidly his faith in mixed farming had been justified was to buy the reasonably priced quarter section that adjoined our place; with it he could double his potential income and at the same time take a long step toward the spacious farm of his dreams. He dismissed the idea when he remembered his promise to build the house in LeRoss. Fortunately for him, the vindication remained to nurture his faith. In every direction he saw further proof, not only of his own hopes for the settlement of the West, but of actual progress toward its fulfillment. The mainline C.P.R., now almost a quarter of a century old, had been augmented by a branch line north of the Qu'Appelle Valley; the site of the village of Lipton promised welcome satisfaction to the first settler father had met. A line through the valley served the Fort, and now the Grand Trunk Pacific was linking Melville to the east with Saskatoon to the northwest, with a village site surveyed for every six or seven miles, including LeRoss. It linked the historic fur traders' Fort Gibraltar, now the City of Winnipeg, with all the proposed new grain elevators that would bring markets within a day's journey of every farmer in the municipality of Kelross. Old-timers he met recalled the Northwest Rebellion of 1885 and that the Saskatchewan River, until the arrival of the C.P.R., had been the main highway linking Eastern Canada with the Pacific. It was exciting progress for an immigrant who had located the surveyor's marker on his own virgin acres only six years before.

One day he left us children with Mrs. Parker while he drove mother to LeRoss to see the site of the new house. When they returned, they spent hours telling us about it.

LeRoss already had two general stores and the owner of one of them had bought a motor car in Winnipeg; our parents had seen the first motor car in London, its royal passenger the Prince of Wales, later King Edward VII. There was a grain elevator and a red railway station, though we children could imagine a train little better than we could imagine the motor car; our knowledge of trains was largely limited to father's pictures of the engine uncle Jos had driven in southern Africa. They described the plank sidewalks and the lumber yard where father had ordered building materials for the frame house that would have an upstairs; climbing a stair would be a new experience for us. There was a hardware store, the post office, and the school near the municipal office, and there would be a new teacher there in September for Nora and me.

The railway and its blanket stitching telegraph poles and a rumor about a telephone line provided fine proof of progress for every settler. For his wife, a dry goods store with relatively convenient access to everyday necessities meant even more.

The sixth Dominion Day picnic would have been a great success but for Nora's sunstroke. Mother was well enough to enjoy herself, her youngest child now walking. The weather was fine, and we were on our way home, Nora and Sylvia and I on the back seat of the democrat, when Nora began to throw up. At first mother thought she might have eaten too much unaccustomed rich food, but as she became worse during the night, she thought about every possible childish illness, particularly diphtheria and typhoid.

Father had told her about how old Angus Macdonald, the Hudson's Bay Company trader, had saved the life of a grandchild choking from diphtheria by swabbing the phlegm from the child's throat with a sliver cut from a stick in the woodbox, wound with a bit of cotton. Fortunately there was as yet no sign of choking and in the morning, as soon as father wakened, he dispelled her fears about serious illness. He had seen many cases of sunstroke near the equator and clearly that was the trouble now.

With rest and cool compresses on her head, the little patient recovered, though she complained of dizziness for days and was not allowed to go out in the sun for the rest of the summer without a hat.

Soon after Dominion Day, a prominent Eastern American grain buyer and his wife visited us on one of a series of inspection trips. They stayed at our house overnight and where mother slept us all I have since often wondered. After breakfast, when father escorted his guest on a tour of several outstanding farms, mother and her feminine guest hung out a neat line of winceyette squares, knowing the wind would dry and bleach them before the men returned for dinner.

Reliving those pioneer years, I now understand some of the appalling situations faced by city-bred women travelling in unoccupied country for the first time. They did not know about the many generations of nomadic Indian women who had evolved their solutions to intimate feminine problems. Gentile women — and most women in our community were gentiles — were unfamiliar with the *Mikvah* bathhouse used by orthodox Jewish women at the new community near Lipton, though days of travel on a slow jolting wagon alerted them to the advantages of such a ritual bathhouse after menstruation. Lacking all such civilized facilities, they took care of their temporary disposal needs in a pail of water swung under the wagon box — just as they did with the baby's diapers. It was an item seldom, if ever, mentioned in every settler's carefully selected list of personal effects.

Women solved the problem of riding skirts in much the same practical manner. Those accustomed to riding side saddle adopted breeches or wore a pair of their husband's tough denim — *serge de Nimes* — overalls, topped by a matching man's smock. They exchanged their familiar divided drawers for knickers, and many a woman — when she had time to think about it — lamented the lack of lace and embroidered cambric and the convenience of garments joined only at the front of the waist band. We knew something about that at an early age because mother insisted that little girls be properly dressed as well as learning to sit properly; divided drawers she said, were for ladies and not for little girls.

The sun shone high and the wind had moderated when father and his guest drove into the yard for dinner after their inspection trip. We had a wild raspberry steamed pudding for dessert — the raspberries Nora and I had helped to pick — one of the steamed suet puddings that always reminded father of holidays on the farm near the Oxford Vale of Aylesbury. With it, mother served a jug of rich cream, a further nostalgic reminder for him.

After dinner, when the men sat smoking their pipes, father found a congenial listener for his philosophical theories about farming and a farmer's life.

The farmer, father said, had always had to take his chances on good or poor crops, good or poor prices; it had been so since the beginning of sowing and harvesting, and probably always would be; the rest of the world got the best of the farmer who had little control over the elements, or, in father's day, markets. The price paid for his produce naturally slumped when the quality and quantity increased. This had been so in England as well as in Saskatchewan, and probably in the United States. But there was much more to a farmer's life. In father's words:

"He must take his compensations elsewhere than from the money marts. He finds them rather in the freedom that comes from contacts with the open spaces and the soil; in his independence of living. No matter how hard he may have to work for that independence so completely unknown to the man who lives in congested communities, he has the supreme satisfaction of enjoying the fruits of his own endeavor."

It was an experience, father maintained, akin to that enjoyed by the true artist. His hands had sowed the seed that nature grew just as the artist applied color to his canvas. He would not lightly exchange it for any other life.

As he harvested his seventh crop, though the first had been no more than a few vegetables, he was clearly savoring the life of his choosing, as he had enjoyed the life in Africa that he had described in the diary he kept for the Mary Eleanor he even then had chosen to share his life with him. Though events, largely mother's health in his estimation, had dictated the family's future move to LeRoss, he had every intention of continuing to develop the homestead as our real home.

The Eternal Feminine

How a woman in the last weeks of pregnancy managed to move into an unfinished house, look after four children and start two of them to school as well as adjust to entirely new surroundings is yet another page in the annals of pioneer prairie life. It could be repeated with variations thousands of times. Even so, that woman fared immeasureably better than most of her peers.

LeRoss was not London or Winnipeg. It was new and raw and in many ways as ugly and utilitarian as the old stable had been. But its rough plank sidewalk that paralleled the Grand Trunk Pacific Railway linked together services and amenities that hitherto in mother's pioneer experience had been entirely lacking.

On the site that five years earlier had been as virginal as father's quarter section when he pitched the tent on the knoll, now there were neighbors within hailing distance, almost two hundred of them including the children. On the day we arrived, Mrs. Hall, whose husband kept the hardware store, brought us an entire meal. Others arrived later with freshly baked bread and pies. They were kind, as neighbors had been on the farm, but for mother their lights shone clearly through the night. The nearest neighbor suggested that she put a light in her own as-yet-uncurtained kitchen window if she ever needed help. If she had not been so overwhelmed with all that had to be done before the hour of her lying-in, mother would have wept tears of gratitude.

Father arrived with Mrs. McPherson on his second Sunday with us, and with not much time to spare. With Mrs. McPherson in charge and the precious harvest waiting, he had few qualms about leaving early the next morning; it was mother's fifth confinement and no complications were expected. The birth of Elfreda Eileen on the twenty-ninth of August was the routine arrival of another baby girl and not the son he had so lightly teased mother about that day they would never forget.

None of those new neighbors delighted mother more than our first teacher, a Nova Scotian who widened our awareness of a country that stretched from the Atlantic Ocean to the Pacific. With imagination and competent tact Miss Lake developed the unorthodox lessons we had learned at home, and filled in many of the obvious gaps. She taught us, along with her other pupils, much about Canada that our parents had had no opportunity to know. Later in the year, she showed us how to skate on the slough where a couple of big boys swept the snow from a patch of ice and built a blazing fire beside the log where we took off our moccasins.

Yet, much as we enjoyed the skating and other games with our new playmates, we continued to enjoy many of our most absorbing games at home, all games that cost no financial outlay and all inspired by mother's ingenuity.

My own favorite for rainy days or when the weather was too cold for us to play in the snow depended on the Eaton's catalogue that now arrived regularly; Eaton's catalogues were never casually thrown away but hoarded as though they were real books or musical scores. It was a strange game for a child who had never seen beautifully furnished rooms or items of fine furniture, and those catalogues could never have been considered arbiters of good taste. With a spare scribbler, a pair of blunt scissors, and a pot of homemade flour-and-water paste, I spent countless hours furnishing rooms with cut-out tables and chairs and curtains and weird objects of art. My only guidance as I arranged and rearranged the sitting rooms and dining rooms, bedrooms and kitchens, and even entrance halls came from equally precious old-country magazines and newspapers, with many a suggestion from mother when she could spare a moment.

We derived much the same pleasure — and learned as much — from the piano father bought when his 1910 crop yielded as well as the oats and barley he had salvaged from the hail storm.

I don't know what Nora and I had expected mother to do with a piano; our only experience with a piano had been watching Mrs. Jonas play on the rare occasions when we visited her home.

Mother looked at it longingly and propped scores on the rack. She placed a picture on top on a small Victorian gilt easel. When father urged her to sit down and play something, to try it out, she looked at her hands, red and chilblained, gnarled from rubbing dirty clothes and sheets and towels on the washboard. She tried to flex her fingers, and she held them up for him to look at. Instead of seating herself as I came to imagine her at the piano in the London home, she turned to him and buried her face against his shoulder — just as she had done when he presented her with the gramophone, now on its little table in the new sitting room.

It was months before she actually attempted to play. In the meantime she stretched her hands and flexed her fingers whenever she could and asked the young neighbor who was a graduate of the Toronto School of Music to give me lessons. From the kitchen or when nursing Freda or brushing someone's hair, she taught me my earliest lessons in discipline in the daily practicing I abhorred. Instead of more scales than she knew I could accept there were simple versions of Handel's "Largo"; "The Evening Star" from *Tannhäuser;* the overture from *The Chimes of Normandy;* Grieg, and *The Bohemian Girl;* simple Etudes, and Schubert's "Ave Maria." Occasionally she sat beside me, and if I had been older I would then have realized how intensely she wanted one of her children to do what she could no longer do to her satisfaction.

In many ways our second winter in LeRoss made up for our parents' differences and mother's hardships.

During the summer months father spent so much time on the farm that occasionally we did not see him for weeks. He had been fortunate in his choice of a man to live in the log house where he kept his own room and shared meals with the tenant and his equally competent wife. Merely to be there made him happy. The 1911 harvest was so good that it renewed his longing to acquire that adjacent quarter section. When the John Deere Company needed a replacement for its agent, a job that could largely be handled during the winter months, and the municipality was ready to replace his services with a full-time secretary-treasurer, he saw a means of raising the capital necessary to cover the asking price — now eight dollars an acre. He had used and liked the company's implements, including the new plough, and he enjoyed meeting farmers who kept him in touch with events around the countryside. The fact that mother was thoroughly involved in village activities relieved him of any feeling that he should discuss with her what really had been his major object in accepting the agency.

For the first time since coming to Canada she had time and a modest opportunity to enjoy her own special interests. Sylvia, soon to start going to school, and Dorothy could safely be put out to play in the well-fenced yard. The baby was weaned. The arrival of Mr. Hilton to take over full-time duties for the municipality was as opportune for her as for father. The new secretary-treasurer had sung as an amateur in London musical halls and knew most of her favorites. When they discovered that they had each performed in the Gilbert and Sullivan one-act *Cox and Box* for which mother had the score, he suggested they rehearse it for a performance in the school.

That was when she propped her scores against the kitchen window while she washed dishes or prepared vegetables, memorizing again long-forgotten lines and tunes. She never looked happier or more lovely than when she swayed rhythmically to her imagined accompaniment, with a dish towel or paring knife in hand.

The show in the school room was a huge success with the borrowed piano and sheets strung on wires for a curtain to give it a suggestion of professionalism. Mr. Hilton ingeniously contrived props and lighting.

Extra seats were brought in and, at twenty-five cents admission, the school's first library received sufficient funds to make a modest beginning. Because the event was so popular and because for so many people from the surrounding country as well as the village it was the best entertainment they had seen in years, it ran for a second evening.

Box socials followed, each woman having decorated an old shoe box or a reminder of a hat shop far away with tissue paper and artificial flowers and bows. Each filled her box with sandwiches and cold meat and chicken and pies and cakes enough for her own family and for the man who would acquire it at auction. Much to mother's amusement, the young man who hoped he had paid a top price for the teacher's contribution, instead won not only hers but with it her five children; he was as game about it as every other man in the hot, congested room. We children were taken home to bed before the fiddle and the piano led off the dancing with *The Merry Widow* waltz.

When mother was happy we children were happy, too, even when we could not quite hear all the music after we were put to bed because now we slept upstairs. When she was unhappy we, too, were unhappy, and one of our saddest days occurred when the *Free Press* brought the news of the tragic sinking of the *Titanic*. Mother imagined every harrowing hour as the great liner sank beneath the icy waves with hundreds of people while the band played "Nearer My God to Thee." Her happy mood began to return only when father announced that he must go to Winnipeg to meet the plough company people, and that he was taking her with him for a holiday. They would go the week after haying and soon after the school holidays commenced.

Dismayed with the unexpected suggestion that she go away on a trip, mother protested that she could not leave five children, especially during the holidays when we all needed special supervision. When father assured her that Mrs. McPherson would come to stay with us, she reminded him that she had nothing suitable to wear; that she had had no new clothes — except the length of chiffon — for eight years; she could not travel in chiffon even if she did make herself a gown. He said this would be her opportunity to buy whatever she wanted. She mentioned the expense. He talked about boarding the train and she said she felt as shy as an awkward school girl. But in the end she left us with more obvious delight in the holiday than actual worry about how we would fare with the trusted Mrs. McPherson.

In Winnipeg they stayed at a real hotel instead of at the Immigration Hall. When they returned home, she had done her hair in a new style, still parted to one side but twisted into three becoming coils at the nape of her neck. But it was the long narrow skirt with the slit to one side that intrigued us children. We had never seen a lady wearing a skirt that showed some of her leg. Nor had we ever seen a hat as wide and beautiful as the hat she admitted was utterly impractical for prairie winds. She never wore it more than a couple of times.

The hat did something for her. It made her feel and look gay and happy, or it may be that we thought it did. That summer, though actually only the month of August remained of our school holidays, for me remains a lovely blur of happiness. She spent hours making dresses for us from the yards of pretty material she brought from Winnipeg, all trimmed with braid or colorful embroidery stitches. She cut bouquets of the huge white sweet peas father grew in the garden during his weekends, and they filled the sitting room with fragrance. She strolled through the bluff to see the pungent clumps of yellow lady's slippers Nora and I found beside a slough. Several times she took us all, Sylvia and Dorothy included with Freda in the pram, for walks along the rough plank sidewalk where we gazed happily at the wonderful displays in the two windows of the two little general stores.

While we played tag and run-sheep-run during the long evenings she often sat at the piano. Usually she played some of the pieces I was trying to learn. At the time I rather resented those reminders, but now whenever I hear them they evoke memories of that unforgettable summer. The sweetly acrid fragrance of wolf willow also brings them back, and the sight of a prairie rose. Just the melody, the few bars that prick childhood memories. The realization that those simplified tunes were each a part of some complete, complex work occurred long after to add another dimension to the treasure. When she sang to her own accompaniment, the songs became a part of our new, exciting life, like the *Kyrie* hanging in the new window, newly framed with the gold-colored *passe partout* from Winnipeg.

It all seemed to end one dusky evening when Nora and I sat on the steps, hugging our knees, savoring the extra minutes before we must go in to bed. Tomorrow, school commenced again, and we were to take Sylvia with us.

It was to be our third year at school, her first. We did not realize that Miss Lake had accomplished something close to miracles in that one-room school. Her pupils — the number varied between sixteen and twenty — also varied in age from first graders of six, such as our little sister, to a big boy of sixteen. Her discipline was very nearly complete: though we sat in pairs in seats for two, only rarely did an inventive boy lock a little girl's long hair into his ink well behind her or, as one did to me, hide a garter snake behind my scribblers where its only escape would be to wriggle on to my lap. It was a clever girl who managed to exchange notes with her friend in the next row without being detected. Miss Lake seldom used the strap. That, as she understood, would have led to charges of favoritism because, while she could easily insist on a small child holding out her reluctant palm, it would have been ridiculous with a hostile youth whose six feet of healthy muscle towered above her.

In many ways it was Tom Sawyer and Huckleberry Finn repeated: capable boys found themselves actually wanting to leave home early enough to start the fire in the Quebec heater by eight o'clock in the morning and regarded it as a privilege. Others swept the school room floor. We girls cleaned the blackboard and as a special treat stencilled the wreaths of down-east autumn maple leaves or Hallowe'en pumpkins or Christmas holly that wreathed them around the changing seasons; there could have been no more acceptable way to extend our horizons beyond prairie poplars and wild flowers than those chalk-dusted stencils.

Because Saskatchewan's Department of Education had not yet advanced to the stage where it published the books we used, we had the advantage of excellent Ontario readers. They introduced us to poems we had to memorize such as "To a Skylark" or accustomed us to overcome our shyness as we read aloud from them before the entire class on Friday afternoons. My earliest lesson in bilingualism came with the story entitled *The Last Lesson in French* and a glimpse of what war, in this case the Franco-Prussian War, could inflict on innocent people.

Each day, we Wilkins children would rush home to tell mother all about what we had formally learned or, when we had completed our own lessons, picked up from Miss Lake's classes for very senior grade-eight pupils or the remarkable student working toward grade twelve.

That autumn I had more than ever before to tell her. Though I had commenced school so much later than she wished — that in itself was not unusual because most of the children in that new school in the newly settled area about LeRoss had had to wait for it — so competent was Miss Lake's teaching that I had caught up to the other children of my own age. But though mother had been so eager to share our childish games and activities all during the holidays, that autumn she seemed to have changed; something had gone out of her gaiety. Sometimes, instead of finding her waiting for us at the door, we found her sitting in the rocking chair. She was often very quiet.

Father had noticed the change, and it worried him. That September he harvested his third successive good crop. With the two earlier good crops he had reminded himself of the frost and the hail that could strike again. The better prices he had received for his grain might not continue. He might not always have such a competent couple to look after the farm; the man had already mentioned that he wanted some day to own his own place. But with a third successful harvest, father allowed himself to savor his achievement. The future looked bright, almost as bright as his hopes had been when he made the heady decision to emigrate. At last he could actually afford to buy that coveted second quarter section, and the time had come when he must tell mother about it.

Several times he found himself rehearsing in his mind how he would break the news to her. He dreaded a scene such as the one that had forced him to move us to LeRoss, or even that August day when she had talked with such conviction about the necessity for schooling. She had enjoyed her little holiday and because she enjoyed it so fully, so did he. The business mission had been highly successful, and he could continue with the implement company agency for as many winters as he chose.

But lately not only had her gaiety seemed forced, her color was too high and her eyes too bright. He wondered if too much excitement might add to whatever was troubling her if, of course, this was not all in his imagination. A sort of unusual apprehension warned him that her slimness might mean that she was much too thin, too fragile, as Mrs. Parker had one day remarked.

Yet it was silly, this anxiety over a conversation with his wife. He knew he had done the right thing for us all, even if she did not realize the fact. If it disturbed her, she would get over her feelings. She must, because that was the way it would always be — the farm every year becoming larger and better equipped and more successful.

To his amazement mother listened to his recital of the facts he had assembled in his mind with scarcely a comment. When he had said it all, she smiled and reached across and touched his hand; she said she hoped that everything would turn out as he planned; if he felt he needed the second quarter section, he knew better than she did.

Her acquiescence troubled father more than open hostility would have done. Briefly, he wondered if, now that she had won her way about our schooling and left the farm, she was completely satisfied; she had her piano and the gramophone; neighbors and a modern house in which some day he planned to install a real bathroom.

Throughout the Sunday with us he watched her, anxious to learn what had caused her changed attitude. She was in no other way changed from the wife he knew, no other way that he could detect except those brief bursts of gaiety that seemed excessive, that high color, and her thinness. Once or twice she seemed close to tears and, though it was a real possibility, he hesitated to upset her by suggesting that she might again be pregnant.

But something was amiss. When he kissed us before leaving to return to the farm, he said he would come back for certain next Saturday — he was bringing in the first load of grain — and he wanted us children all to be at home.

It was all most unusual. He never came home from the farm on Saturday morning and before he appeared he had already stabled his team at the livery near the west end of the village and close to the elevator. Half an hour later a strange democrat driven by a strange young man with a strange team drew up beside the gate.

Father introduced him to us children and to mother as a doctor.

None of us children knew anything about doctors; Nora and I certainly could not remember the doctor who attended us before we left

England. Father explained that he had met him while on business in the next village and that we were fortunate that he could spare enough time in LeRoss to see us; he would not hurt us at all.

We children were very subdued by the unusual situation. Mother said little as father explained that the doctor was a recent graduate from an eastern medical school who planned to spend a few years in the West while he acquired experience and, father added with an understanding smile, enough funds to undertake post-graduate studies.

The doctor gave each of us children a brief, cursory examination and then he examined mother. He spent a long time with her, and he asked her and father many questions. Before he left he confirmed what father had feared as he had quietly watched her during the past few weeks. That high color, the abnormal gaiety and moods of excitement and occasional uncharacteristic bursts of passion were symptoms of the euphoria and depression that were often associated with T.B., consumption.

The young doctor, who had attended lectures by the famous Dr. William Osler, explained that tuberculosis was not now the hopeless disease that for centuries had terrified all who had contracted it; with rest and proper medicine many persons recovered completely. He recommended that we move to some center where mother could be near experienced doctors who would give her the treatment she needed, perhaps to a higher altitude and a drier climate where there were not so many bluffs. The alternative, he advised, would be prolonged treatment in a sanitarium.

That night father and mother were still talking downstairs when we went to sleep, and though it was Sunday he had left next morning before we wakened. Mother told us that we were going to move; she did not know where but it would be to a larger town where there would be a much larger school and more than one teacher; that wherever we went there would be a high school where, when we had completed our public school education, we could learn more than at LeRoss. Nothing about herself. Nothing that might indicate that she was far from well.

She was alone with us children for two entire weeks, the loneliest, most terrifying fortnight of several during her thirty-eight years. In a strange coincidence, on her birthday she recalled that day eight years ago when father welcomed her into the log house. It was an era that was coming to an end. She knew it only in her bones and because the future, their future, was a murky, fearful unknown. Night after night she told herself that nothing was ever as bad as she had expected it to be, that her premonitions always loomed larger than the situations they foretold.

She was not the kind of woman who would frighten her children with possibilities we could not understand. Even I, the eldest, could know nothing about the story behind *La Bohème,* and nothing, either, of the significance of Mimi's last tragic aria. In spite of the shortages and handicaps of our upbringing so far, we five had always been cherished and protected.

But while she had protected and cherished us, she had seldom spared herself. Now, unreasonably, she blamed herself for letting father down, for failing to support him as he needed. All her regrets about her lack of physical stamina, coupled with her determination that his life as a farmer should not deny his children the advantages she wanted for us — and knew that he, too, in his heart wanted — swirled through her mind. As more than one dawn brightened and finally lighted the choristers in their procession she recalled the words of the "Kyrie" they sang:

"Lord have mercy upon us. . . ."

As the days and nights dragged on, her anxiety about why he did not come home heightened her feeling that if they were together she could offer some sort of solution. She longed for some way by which he could continue the life he loved, short of returning to England or any other desperate separation. That was what she dreaded above every other possibility she could imagine, being parted from him. She might even have accepted the possibilities more easily if she had not felt so much better during the past few months.

Visits to Mrs. Hall, now the dearest friend she had known in Canada, helped to cheer her momentarily. She read to Nora and me at bedtime, and sang to us all. She walked the path we had made through the bluff on our way to school and chatted with Miss Lake; gathered the last autumn flowers in the garden, and each morning before the frosts withered every green leaf, garnered in the remaining vegetables. And each day she had to drive herself to do whatever she did.

She recovered her zest and strength miraculously when father returned. His tired eyes and the tight lines about his mouth told her that he, too, had spent sleepless, troubled nights and though the new hurt look worried her, it drew him closer. For only a moment they clung desperately to one another, and then he picked up Freda and tossed her high, and ruffled Dodie's hair and Sybbie's and wanted to know how Nora and I had got on at school. After supper, when we were in bed, he would tell her all his news.

His first momentous news was that he had sold the farm — the land, the house and other buildings, and the animals and implements. Everything except the crop that would see us through the next few months, he hoped. No mention of the quarter section he had planned to buy; that would cause her too much distress. He had persuaded the tenant to buy the farm, parting with it completely because if he rented it he could not bear the thought of another man doing what he longed to do.

All without consulting her because he knew too well that so momentous a decision would add to her already strained emotions.

"I had said good-bye to the land," he told us many years later when he could talk about it. "I had assumed the yoke of the indoors.

"We could pay our bills, and buy many things we needed. Most of all, we could buy freedom forever for those of the family for whom the drudgery, invariably done generously and without complaint, had extracted too great a toll of energy and spirit." Fortunately, he never knew — as I discovered later — that the house and stable and granaries were bulldozed by a subsequent owner to enlarge a great field of wheat that waved over and above the beloved little knoll.

Did he relinquish it all because he remembered how gallantly she had tried to accept the life he had chosen? Because of his love that had grown and deepened since their African separation? Anguish over the fate that threatened not only her but all of us? Had he parted with the independence he craved, the freedom and challenge of a farmer's life because something akin to Goethe's "the eternal feminine draws us on" had urged him to take so drastic a course? Or had he realized that unless he acted quickly and completely, the vestiges of his Victorian dedication to splendid sacrifice might succumb to the mundane advice of the ancient Yorkshire adage he had so often heard as a boy: let not your bleeding heart run away with your bloody head?

Like every individual blessed with loyalty and affection for both parents, I shall always want and never know the answers to those queries.

Nor do I know the answers to the appalling questions that mother must have asked herself. Nor the extent to which she understood and appreciated the sacrifice he had made. The extent of his awareness of all it might mean to him and to us children.

Against all the unknowns, I know that some time soon after his return and his enormous sacrifice, mother again became pregnant. Whether on account of the then still prevalent old wives' belief that pregnancy was a palliative if not a cure for consumption or contemporary ignorance of the cause of the disease and its prognosis, the situation seems to have caused little serious concern. But I can so easily understand their need for one another that had grown and matured with the years; the dependence of two so different people on what each had brought to the other; the brief moment of physical delight and forgetfulness that provided the greatest comfort mother could imagine and from which over the years she had found hope and courage and insight.

The other news he had to share on his return that late September was that he had been to Regina for a couple of days. Faced with the urgent necessity of finding some means of supporting us all now that he no longer relied on the farm, and because he had few opportunities to know about openings in the province, he had looked to the few men he knew in the government for information and guidance. It had not even occurred to him to consider leaving Western Canada, nor to think about returning to England. His choice of location was Swift Current, a small city of five thousand in the southwestern corner of Saskatchewan, already an established distributing center. The climate was said to be dry and bracing. There was a new hospital and several resident doctors, modern telephone services, and electricity.

Father had written to the Swift Current Board of Trade about possible openings for the photography that was his first and natural choice of occupation. Unfortunately, as he told mother, before he could have received a reply, he had learned in Regina that an able Welsh photographer was already established and very popular. His next choice came from his former employment with the London firm of R. and J. Beck, world-famous manufacturers of optical lenses, the firm that had supplied his African photographic equipment by way of the port of Durban. The optical supply house in Winnipeg he had heard of on his trips to the Manitoba capital had encouraged him to go ahead with the lens manufacturing plant about which he had consulted them.

Our future was settled. Father would go ahead to Swift Current late in March, get his plant started, and find a house to which we could move as soon as mother recovered from her sixth confinement.

Mrs. McPherson came again late in June. It was her fourth time. Mother had arrived in LeRoss just before her last confinement and was to leave as soon as she could following another. She badly needed the assistance Mrs. McPherson willingly provided with sorting and packing the accumulation of settler's effects and household possessions acquired during almost a decade, all having to be crated for shipment by train.

Late one evening at the end of the first week in July, Nora and I skipped over with her to see Mrs. Hall, leaving the competent midwife to put the three little ones to bed. I am glad we went with her on that pleasant stroll, one clinging to either hand, otherwise I should not have heard her words to her friend as she said good-night.

"Come over in the morning and see my son!"

Again, she had been too optimistic. During the night she gave birth to her sixth daughter and she knew then that father would never have his son. Yet, as long as she lived, he had a poignant reminder of mother in Grace Bernice who grew up to inherit mother's lovely body and the eyes that so often seemed too large for her face — and also her frail health.

Father had already offered the LeRoss house for sale, and the piano because it was going to cost so much to pack and ship it, generously promising mother another when we were settled in Swift Current; it was the same promise he had made prior to their departure from the Highgate villa.

Late in August we moved to the village hotel while the furniture was packed, along with the souvenirs of Africa and London, and the gramophone and records. Then, with the six-week-old baby in her arms, alone with her five other children all under twelve, mother boarded the train for an overnight change at Melville and, crossing the Qu'Appelle Valley and the Touchwood Trail by another railway line, yet another connection westward from Regina.

L'envoi

Swift Current was all mother could have wished for us children and for father, too, now that he had sacrificed his farm and his dream. Though it was new and raw and alien to the prairie that was so incredibly lovely when we got to know it, compared with LeRoss it was a miniature London. It offered her most of the amenities she had so often longed for and so many of the everyday, practical assets that she needed.

Instead of having to clean lamp chimneys and trim wicks and fill lamp bowls with coal oil, at the flick of a switch every room in the house could be flooded with light. Instead of peering through the window for a glimpse of father's stable lamp, as far as she could see every street was bright with light that came from the power house across the tracks from the grain elevators. She could hardly believe that for years she had searched through the night for some proof that there was anyone else in the world beyond her own log house.

At the sink in the kitchen water came from a tap. There was water in the bathroom and a real W.C. The task she had easily accepted when she felt well, and indeed welcomed after a winter storm — carrying in the snow that she melted for water — would no longer make her feel inadequate; it no longer existed. Some day, father said, there would be an electric cooking stove as efficient as the gas stove in their Highgate kitchen; with no supply of firewood within hundreds of miles, even that wonderful furnace in the cellar might some day burn coal or even natural gas from a well larger than the first tiny outlet south of town along the Swift Current creek.

Two elementary schools were ready to enroll us in September, with a dozen teachers. The red brick, eight-room Collegiate Institute would be completed next year. There was a library where we could borrow as many books as we could read. A modern telephone in father's office linked him, and us, with people all across the country. One Saturday afternoon he took Nora and me to our very first moving picture show, the serialized *Million Dollar Mystery,* and later he and mother took us to the Princess Royal, a real theater where travelling players offered road shows from time to time and where one-act plays such as mother's *Cox and Box* might be professionally presented.

While mother was too busy settling our new home to explore the marvels of Swift Current, we older children soon found our way to the stores on Central Avenue, our greedy young appetites often painfully tempered by father. Every day, it seemed, he had to remind us that he had only recently established himself in the booming distributing center for southwestern Saskatchewan. We often needed the reminder. Vitally important as mother considered our new school, we were also learning about banana splits — three scoops of ice cream topped with strawberry jam and nuts and chocolate and whipped cream and available in both the Greek and Chinese restaurants; curly white sheepskin tippets and muffs on a cord that went over your head; toys and sparkling bits of jewelry; red apples too casually spilling over the barrel in front of the small general store we passed on our way to school. The many kinds of colored candies we ogled from the buyer's side of big glass jars and display cases taught us much that she had not yet thought about. There was so much, he reminded us, that he could not yet afford.

We also went to church for the first time in a real church, and to Sunday School. During the winter we tobogganed down Central Avenue hill and skated on the frozen creek that meandered under the railway tracks on its way north to join the South Saskatchewan River; it was another first experience because we had never before seen water that flowed instead of remaining in a slough until the sun evaporated it.

The following summer we found huge yellow cactus flowers on the sun-facing slope of a coulee, flowers that, mother said, would delight a Paris milliner. We picnicked at the lone tree near the little dam that collected Swift Current's water supply. The lone tree was another marvel because the only other trees in or near the prairie city were the hundreds of saplings taking root along the residential streets and in front of some of the larger, more imposing houses.

We had so many children to play with that we could not remember all of their names when mother asked us about them. Often there was a wistful note in her voice when she enquired about their mothers.

That was the tragedy that mocked our move to Swift Current and that became apparent to us older children following the evening of the declaration of war. Despite the medicine and rest prescribed by Dr. McLean, mother's health did not improve. Old Angelique took over the washing and a neighbor came to do the mending and sewing. But still there were six children clamoring for her attention every day.

That August 4, 1914 had been a day of excitement, though no one seemed to know why. They had merely felt something in the air, all except the editor and publisher of the local newspaper and the few men who received telegrams alerting them to report to their reserve or regular regiments. When dusk fell the Salvation Army band played at the corner of Central Avenue and Cheadle Street, martial music and hymns with a fine, noisy marching rhythm such as "Onward Christian Soldiers." Father went downtown after supper to see what was happening but when he asked mother if she wanted to go with him, she said she thought she ought to stay at home with us children.

She had stayed at home because she was too tired to go with him, as she longed to do. When he returned, instead of finding her standing in the street with her neighbors, she was sitting in the rocking chair beside the new electric lamp with the Tiffany glass shade.

She asked him about the war and how it could affect people living so far from Germany and Belgium and England. They talked about what it might mean to their friends and families at home, to the local men who, father had heard, had just been called up for reserve or active service. Suddenly, without warning, the light in the lamp beside her flickered and went out. So did the light in the little hallway. As they both got up to find their way for a candle they always kept in readiness for such an emergency, they realized that every light in the street had also gone, and every light in every neighbor's house. Not a light remained in the entire town except a strange glow from the vicinity of the grain elevators near the power house. From the open door father exclaimed, as if he could not believe what he saw; the big grain elevator was on fire. Obviously, because the flames were already shooting high and out from one side of the structure, they had cut the main power lines. Swift Current lay dark among its low, sheltering hills, so dark that even the stars failed to shine out against the one, terrifying source of light.

Women's voices shrieked hysterically as the new fire wagon raced through the streets, its siren heightening the shocking drama. People who ran toward the blazing elevator, hoping to get a better look, found themselves blocked by a rope hastily stretched between a couple of scarlet uniformed officers and the local constables. Travelling faster than the fire wagon, rumors raced through the streets: the two other elevators would catch fire if the wind changed; there was not enough water pressure in the hydrants; the wind was already changing; the entire town was threatened and everyone had better prepare to evacuate it and cross over the creek for the only possible safety.

The excitement was more than mother's dwindling strength could stand. Though the wind did not change and the great monolith burned to its foundation without spreading to the other elevators, she collapsed before the lights came on again. It was only a brief, not terribly frightening collapse, but she never completely recovered.

Father moved us to the brown house on Third Avenue East across from where Dr. McLean lived, only a short block from the hospital and with a bathroom and bedroom on the ground floor. Mother got us settled and the furniture in place and the curtains hung before she was forced to take to her bed across from the sitting room. We six children slept upstairs in a large dormitory, and father slept on a couch in the sitting room, without closing the door. The dining room next to the kitchen became our family room, with the gramophone on a table in front of the window, and the records on a handy shelf below it. Mother never got another piano.

With the doctor's reluctant yet sympathetic help, father made every possible provision to keep her at home with us instead of letting her go to a sanitarium.

Last Christmas she had sent photos of the baby to her sisters in England and to friends at Headlands P.O. and LeRoss. Her hand had been firm as she wrote "Grace Bernice, age 5 months, wishing you a merry Christmas from the whole Wilkins family." This year there were no cards, no greetings. Father made a gallant effort at finding presents for us children and at organizing a sort of celebration. Instead of playing games and gathering about a tree, we gathered around mother's bed, father with the baby in his arms. We said some prayers. Mother gave me one of her little satin-lined London jewellers' boxes with five silver coins replacing the earrings it originally had held. She said I must try to look after my sisters; she apparently had forgotten that there were six of us, or assumed that I was too old to want one of the coins, or Grace too young.

Because father could find no housekeeper-practical nurse, I stayed out of school for the remainder of the winter, and old Angelique came twice a week, sometimes oftener, to do the washing. Each morning when he cleaned clinkers from the furnace and filled the monster with fresh coal, father burned the wax-covered, cardboard sputum cups that mother now required, meticulously washing his hands in strong disinfectant before helping me prepare breakfast.

The mornings must have been agony for her as she listened to the sounds of her family awakening; the baby still upstairs and fretful; Freda needing help with her dressing; father announcing that everyone going to school must be out of the house in ten minutes. Yet she smiled when I took her the glass of water for her teeth and the basin and towel for her morning wash.

Instead of my awkward help I knew she longed for father to sit beside her, even for a few minutes before he had to leave for his office, the shopping list in his pocket. For her, every night was worse than every morning as she lay awake with her memories and faced grim facts that nothing could relieve, her sole comfort the knowledge that our education had been assured, that father had made his tough adjustment to a semblance of his former townsman's life; wishing she could have contributed more than six daughters to the splendid family farm life he had hoped for in the New World.

The one bright spot for her during those impotent days was the supper hour when father played her favorite records on the gramophone, carefully avoiding the hopeless "Stars are Shining."

We were having supper later in January when he put the new record on the gramophone, the one he hoped she could hear and knew she would enjoy: Bach's Suite No. 3 in D Major with the "Air on the G String." Minutes after he sat down at the table, suddenly he checked the catch on the baby's high chair beside him, and left us. When he came out of mother's room, father closed the door behind him.

He said we must finish our supper, and got us all upstairs to bed. Then he phoned the doctor and made the inevitable arrangements. She was buried in her nightgown in the lonely little cemetery across the north coulee, still wearing the gold wedding ring he had had made for her in Africa. She was forty-two.